Parables
& Other Bible
Studies

PUBLISHING

Torrance, California

© 2010 Bristol Works, Inc.
Rose Publishing, Inc.
4733 Torrance Blvd., #259
Torrance, California 90503 U.S.A.
Email: info@rose-publishing.com
www.rose-publishing.com

Includes these Rose Publishing Titles:

Parables of Jesus © 2010 Bristol Works, Inc.
    Contributing Authors: Benjamin Galan, MTS, ThM; Vincent Botticelli
Life of Joseph © 2010 Bristol Works, Inc.
    Author: Benjamin Galan, MTS, ThM
Esther © 2009 Bristol Works, Inc.
    Author: Benjamin Galan, MTS, ThM
Proverbs © 2010 Bristol Works, Inc.
    Author: Benjamin Galan, MTS, ThM
Life of David © 2009 Bristol Works, Inc.
    Author: Benjamin Galan, MTS, ThM
Dare to Love: 1 Corinthians 13 © 2009 Bristol Works, Inc.
    Contributing Authors: William Brent Ashby, BT; Benjamin Galan, MTS, ThM
Psalm 23 © 2008 Bristol Works, Inc.
    Contributing Authors: William Brent Ashby, BT; Benjamin Galan, MTS, ThM

Many of these titles are available as individual pamphlets, as wall charts, and as ready-to-use PowerPoint® presentations.

All Scripture quotations, unless otherwise noted, are taken from the *Holy Bible, New International Version®. NIV®.* Copyright © 1973, 1978, 1984 by International Bible Society. Used by permission of Zondervan. All rights reserved.

Library of Congress Cataloging-in-Publication Data

Parables and other favorite Bible studies.
    p. cm. – (Rose Bible basics)
  Summary: "Bible studies on common Old & New Testament characters and topics"–Provided by publisher.
  Includes bibliographical references and index.
  ISBN 978-1-59636-416-5 (pbk. : alk. paper)
  1. Bible–Introductions. I. Rose Publishing (Torrance, Calif.)
  BS475.3.P355 2010
  220.6'1–dc22
                        2010023239

Printed by Regent Publishing Services Ltd.
Printed in China
July 2010, First printing

Parables
& Other Bible Studies

Contents

Continued
on next
page

Parables

& Other Bible Studies

Contents

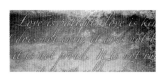

Parables
of Jesus

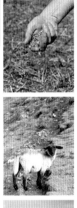

39 Stories Jesus Told

How to Read Parables

Stories Jesus Told

Word Pictures

Metaphor: Comparison of two objects, emphasizing a specific similarity or similarities. When the psalmist affirms that "God is my rock" (Ps. 18:2, 31; 42:9), we should not understand that God is literally a rock. Rather, the psalmist is comparing a specific characteristic of rocks with a specific characteristic of God. That is, just as rocks are solid and strong, so is God.

Simile: Like a metaphor, a simile is a comparison between two objects. However, the comparison is more evident, which makes the comparison more emphatic and vivid. Similes use the words *as* and *like* to make the comparison between the two objects obvious. When the psalmist writes, "man is like a breath," (Ps. 144:4) the comparison is direct and clear. The parables of the kingdom of God that begin with "the kingdom of God (or heaven)" are examples of similes.

Allegory: An allegory is an extended metaphor. It refers to stories, poems, images, and words that convey meanings beyond the literal one. An example of an intended allegory in the New Testament is found in Gal. 4:21–31, in which Sarah and Hagar stand for two covenants.

Jesus' parables are among the most read and loved sections of the Bible. Just as in the times of Jesus, the parables are filled with vivid images and touch the readers in powerful ways. In short, the parables have been an important source of wisdom, instruction, and solace for Christians everywhere.

In the following pages, we will understand what parables are, what they do in the Gospels, and why they matter so much to us today. We will also learn some general suggestions for reading the parables fruitfully.

What Are Parables?

Parables are stories that fulfill a specific function in a specific way. Parables are extended analogies. In other words, parables are extended comparisons between two objects. This comparison seeks to identify similarities or highlight differences to explain or clarify something about one of the objects. Some parables are extended similes or extended metaphors, others are brief allegories. This means that in our reading of the parables, we must be careful to not interpret the metaphors, similes, and allegories beyond what the Bible itself allows.

Parables in the Gospels

	Parable	Matthew	Mark	Luke
1	A Lamp on a Stand	Matt. 5:14–16	Mark 4:21–22	Luke 8:16–17; 11:33–36
2	The Wise and Foolish Builders	Matt. 7:24–27		Luke 6:47–49
3	New Cloth on an Old Garment	Matt. 9:16	Mark 2:21	Luke 5:36
4	New Wine in Old Wineskins	Matt. 9:17	Mark 2:22	Luke 5:37–38
5	The Sower	Matt. 13:3–9	Mark 4:2–9	Luke 8:4–8
6	The Weeds	Matt. 13:24–30		
7	The Mustard Seed	Matt. 13:31–32	Mark 4:30–32	Luke 13:18–19
8	The Yeast	Matt. 13:33		Luke 13:20–21
9	The Hidden Treasure	Matt. 13:44		
10	The Pearl	Matt. 13:45–46		
11	The Net	Matt. 13:47–50		
12	The Lost Sheep	Matt. 18:12–14		Luke 15:3–7
13	The Unmerciful Servant	Matt. 18:23–35		
14	The Workers in the Vineyard	Matt. 20:1–16		
15	The Two Sons	Matt. 21:28–32		
16	The Tenants	Matt. 21:33–45	Mark 12:1–12	Luke 20:9–19
17	The Wedding Banquet	Matt. 22:2–14		
18	The Ten Virgins	Matt. 25:1–13		
19	The Talents	Matt. 25:14–30		
20	The Growing Seed		Mark 4:26–29	
21	The Absent Householder		Mark 13:34–37	
22	The Creditor and the Two Debtors			Luke 7:41–43
23	The Good Samaritan			Luke 10:30–37
24	A Friend in Need			Luke 11:5–13
25	The Rich Fool			Luke 12:16–21
26	The Watchful Servants			Luke 12:35–40
27	The Faithful Servant	Matt. 24:45–51		Luke 12:42–48
28	The Barren Fig Tree			Luke 13:6–9
29	The Place of Honor			Luke 14:7–11
30	The Great Banquet			Luke 14:16–24
31	The Cost of Being a Disciple			Luke 14:25–35
32	The Lost Coin			Luke 15:8–10
33	The Prodigal Son			Luke 15:11–32
34	The Shrewd Steward			Luke 16:1–13
35	The Rich Man and Lazarus			Luke 16:19–31
36	The Obedient Servant			Luke 17:7–10
37	The Persistent Widow			Luke 18:1–8
38	The Pharisee and the Tax Collector			Luke 18:9–14
39	The Ten Minas			Luke 19:11–27
	Total Parables in each Gospel	20	8	27
	Unique Parables in each Gospel	10	2	17

Title	Summary	Comments
1 *A Lamp on a Stand* Matt. 5:14–16 Mark 4:21–22 Luke 8:16–17; 11:33–36	Jesus declared that his followers are the light of the world. He then asks them not to hide their light, but rather put it on a stand to be effective. 	Christians are called to be light in a darkened world. This involves living according to Christ's commandments and allowing our lives to reflect Jesus' love, obedience, humility, and forgiveness.
2 *The Wise and Foolish Builders* Matt. 7:24–27 Luke 6:47–49	At the conclusion of the Sermon on the Mount (Matt. 5:1–7:29), Jesus contrasts those that understand and do his words with those who do not. A wise person builds upon a rock and endures the storms; a foolish person builds upon sand and suffers loss.	Jesus stresses the importance of having a sure and steady foundation. Scripture tells us that Jesus alone is that worthy foundation (1 Cor. 3:11).
3 *New Cloth on an Old Garment* Matt. 9:16 Mark 2:21 Luke 5:36	Jesus explains the danger of patching a garment with new cloth. Once washed, the new cloth would shrink and make the tear worse.	The parable challenges its audience to understand the newness of Jesus' message. Jesus did not come to get rid of the law but to fulfill it. By fulfilling it, Jesus extends the meaning of the law (love your enemies, for example). The ritual-and-sacrifice faith of the Old Testament would not make room for this type of change. What Jesus offers, then, is a whole "new cloth."
4 *New Wine in Old Wineskins* Matt. 9:17 Mark 2:22 Luke 5:37–38	Jesus refers to the fact that wineskins stretch as the wine they contain ferments. If a wineskin is used again, it is unable to stretch any further and breaks. 	As in the parable of the new cloth on the old garment, this parable also challenges its audience to understand the newness of Jesus' message. Jesus did not come to get rid of the law but to fulfill it. By fulfilling it, Jesus extends the meaning of the law (love your enemies, for example). The ritual-and-sacrifice faith of the Old Testament would not make room for this type of change. What Jesus offers, then, is a whole "new wineskin."

Title	Summary	Comments
The Sower Matt. 13:3–9 Mark 4:2–9 Luke 8:4–8	A farmer spreads seed that falls into four types of soil. Seed that falls on hard soil is eaten by the birds. Seed that falls on rocks springs up quickly, but withers due to lack of root. Seed that falls in weeds is overtaken. Seed that falls in good soil produces much fruit. 	This parable includes an explanation of the four soils as symbolic of the responses of people who hear the proclamation of the kingdom of God. The parable challenges its audience to receive the word about the kingdom of heaven, be focused on that message, and grow. A true hearing of the message of the kingdom of God becomes a productive hearing and productive living.
The Weeds Matt. 13:24–30	A farmer sows good seed but his enemy comes in the night and plants weeds also. The farmer decides to allow them both to grow, planning to separate them at harvest time.	This parable explains the co-existence of believers and unbelievers until the Lord's return (Matt. 13:36–43).
The Mustard Seed Matt. 13:31–32 Mark 4:30–32 Luke 13:18–19	The kingdom of heaven is compared to the mustard seed. This seed, the smallest known to Jesus' audience, becomes so great a bush that birds build their nests in it.	The kingdom does not come as a powerful mustard tree; rather, it arrives as a small seed that grows and provides shade and refuge. The kingdom of God is already present in the ministry of Jesus, but its fullness will only happen when Jesus comes back.
The Yeast Matt. 13:33 Luke 13:20–21	The kingdom of heaven is compared to yeast which, when put in dough, spreads throughout the entire mixture, causing it to expand.	The yeast is symbolic of the growing influence of the kingdom of God on the world (Matt. 28:19–20).
The Hidden Treasure Matt. 13:44	The kingdom of heaven is compared to a found treasure that is so desirable that a man sells all he has to acquire it.	Jesus announces the presence of the kingdom of heaven and invites his audience to rejoice in finding it.
The Pearl Matt. 13:45–46	The kingdom of heaven is compared to a pearl buyer who finds such a desirable pearl that he sells all he has to purchase it.	In this parable, Jesus urges his audience to recognize the value of the kingdom of heaven in their midst.
The Net Matt. 13:47–50	The kingdom of heaven is compared to a net that draws in both good (which is kept) and bad (which is burned).	This parable illustrates the separation of believers from unbelievers when Jesus returns (Matt. 25:32–46).

TITLE	SUMMARY	COMMENTS
12 **The Lost Sheep** Matt. 18:12–14 Luke 15:3–7	When a sheep gets lost, the shepherd searches for the missing sheep and rejoices when he finds it.	The parable invites readers to participate in seeking and to join in celebrating the finding of the lost.
13 **The Unmerciful Servant** Matt. 18:23–35	A king, at his servant's pleading, forgives him of a great debt, which he could never repay. This same servant then imprisons a fellow servant who could not repay a much smaller debt. In response, the king has the first servant imprisoned.	We should be forgiving of others, realizing the great debt we have been forgiven by Christ (Ephesians 2:13).
14 **The Workers in the Vineyard** Matt. 20:1–16	A vineyard owner hires workers at 6 AM for a day's wages to work in his vineyard. At 9 AM, noon, 3 PM and 5 PM he hires additional workers. At 6 PM, he pays them all a full day's wages. The first workers feel cheated, but the owner reminds them that he paid them exactly what they agreed to.	The parable challenges the audience to understand that the way God treats people is not based on human standards of justice. The parable emphasizes God's mercy as the basis for salvation as it forces listeners to confront issues of envy, a sense of superiority, and jealousy.

TITLE	SUMMARY	COMMENTS
15 **The Two Sons** Matt. 21:28–32	A man has two sons, whom he asks to work in his vineyard. The first says he will not, but later regrets it and goes to work. The second says he will work, but does not. The first son is the one that did the father's will.	A contrast of sinners who repent and are saved versus hypocrites who say the right things but do not do them (Ezek. 33:31–32).
16 **The Tenants** Matt. 21:33–45 Mark 12:1–12 Luke 20:9–19	A landowner prepares a vineyard and rents it out to farmers while he goes far away. At harvest time, he sends servants to collect the "rent" (first fruits) but the farmers treat the servants shamefully. He finally sends his son, whom they kill. He will therefore destroy the wicked farmers and rent the vineyard to others.	This is one of the most difficult parables to interpret. The parable does not say that God has rejected the Jewish people as a group. It is an indictment against the Jewish leaders who rejected John the Baptist and Jesus. The parable demands from its audience that they reject, in turn, those leaders and follow Jesus.

TITLE	SUMMARY	COMMENTS
17 **The Wedding Banquet** Matt. 22:2–14	A king prepares a wedding feast for his son and sends for the guests, who all give poor excuses for not attending and even murder his servants. The king destroys those people and invites others to the feast.	An indictment of the Jewish leaders' treatment and rejection of the prophets and Jesus. The offer of salvation is now open to all that will trust in Christ (Acts 28:28).
18 **The Ten Virgins** Matt. 25:1–13	Ten bridesmaids await the arrival of the bridegroom, but only the five that were wise enough to prepare with extra oil for their lamps were ready when he arrived and went with him.	The parable urges people to be ready and prepared for Christ's imminent return.
19 **The Talents** Matt. 25:14–30	Before going on a long trip, a man gives each of his three servants a different sum of his money to invest. Two double the money they were given and are rewarded; the third buries his for no profit and loses reward.	At his return, Christ expects Christians to have used the gifts and opportunities he has given them (Col. 1:10). The central issue of the parable is faithfulness. The parable exhorts its audience to remain faithful disciples of Jesus in the time before his return.
20 **The Growing Seed** Mark 4:26–29	The kingdom of God is compared to seeds that grow to maturity. We do not understand the process of growth the seed experiences. However, when the fruit is ripe, it is harvested.	The parable conveys confidence and comfort to its audience by assuring that the kingdom of God will find fulfillment in God's time. It also reminds us that this fulfillment is inevitable and does not depend on human efforts.
21 **The Absent Householder** Mark 13:34–37	Christ is compared to a homeowner who goes on a trip and leaves his servants in charge. The servants must not be caught idle upon his return.	This brief comparison calls all believers to be ready for the return of Jesus. Being ready means that Christians are occupied with the matters and issues of the kingdom of heaven. Christ has left Christians to do his work in the world as salt and light. Our joy is to be found faithful upon his return (Matt. 5:13).

TITLE	SUMMARY	COMMENTS
22 *The Creditor and the Two Debtors* Luke 7:41–43	A creditor forgives two debtors. One is forgiven an amount ten times greater than the other is. Christ confirms that the one that was forgiven the larger amount will love the creditor more.	As we come to understand more and more how great a debt we have been forgiven, we will love Christ more (Mark 12:30).
23 *The Good Samaritan* Luke 10:30–37	A Jew traveling to Jericho was beaten, robbed, and left for dead. Both a priest and a Levite passed him by, but a Samaritan (hated by the Jews) rescued the man and ensured his recovery.	As a response to, "Who is my neighbor?" Jesus shows that life in the kingdom of God requires us to love our neighbors, even our enemies. The parable is a call to action; love is not only a matter of feelings or thoughts but of actions.
24 *A Friend in Need* Luke 11:5–13	A man goes to his neighbor late at night to ask for bread for a friend who has arrived from a long journey. Although the neighbor initially refuses, he eventually gives in to end the knocking at his door.	This is an encouragement to Christians to continue in prayer with perseverance and hope because God hears prayers and responds.
25 *The Rich Fool* Luke 12:16–21	A rich man has a harvest that will last him many years so he decides to "eat, drink, and be merry." God calls him a fool because that same night he will die and not enjoy his riches.	This brief parable reminds us that wisdom attends to the things of God, while foolishness concerns itself only with this life. We have very little control over life and our own success. God is the source of life, all that we need for that life, and satisfaction with our life.
26 *The Watchful Servants* Luke 12:35–40	A homeowner is pleased when he returns unexpectedly and finds his servants are ready to receive him at any time. Whether it is the master or a thief, the servants ought to be ready for each.	Jesus did not reveal the time of his second coming. Yet, he expects his servants, all Christians, to be ready to receive him when he comes back. The church is ready by doing the work of the kingdom of God and by remaining holy and faithful to Christ.
27 *The Faithful Servant* Luke 12:42–48 Matt. 24:45–51	A master will reward the servant that cares for his duties in the master's absence. Conversely, a master will punish the servant who willfully disregards his duties during his master's absence.	The parable urges its audience to right and wise living. Wisdom, in this parable, is living with the end in mind.

TITLE	SUMMARY	COMMENTS
The Barren Fig Tree Luke 13:6–9	A vineyard owner becomes frustrated because a fig tree has not produced in three years. He commands that it be cut down, but his servant asks for one more year to nurture it. 	The parable demands a response to the privilege of being God's people: Christians must "bear fruit." Bearing fruit in Luke means to live in obedience to God's will. This includes being witnesses, loving our neighbor, doing justice and loving mercy.
The Place of Honor Luke 14:7–11	When someone is invited to a feast, that person is wise to choose a humble place.	The parable confronts its audience with our natural desire to be noticed, loved, and exalted. Yet, Jesus reminded his audience that a wise person understands his own value and place in the kingdom of God (Phil. 2:3).
The Great Banquet Luke 14:16–24	A man prepares a great feast for many people, but when he summons them they have a number of poor excuses for not attending. The man instead invites all the poor and disadvantaged in the city. 	Salvation and the blessings of God are received by those who gladly accept and appreciate his good gifts (James 1:17).
The Cost of Being a Disciple Luke 14:25–35	It is wise to consider the cost before undertaking an important task. A person ensures sufficient funding for a building project. A leader ensures his military might is sufficient before engaging in war.	The parable urges its audience to carefully consider the cost of following Christ: surrendering our all to him and choosing his will over our own (Mark 8:34–35).
The Lost Coin Luke 15:8–10	A woman loses one of ten coins and looks diligently until she finds it. When it is found, she rejoices greatly.	Christ seeks those that are lost, and the inhabitants of heaven rejoice every time a person is saved (John 3:16).

TITLE	SUMMARY	COMMENTS
33 *The Prodigal Son* Luke 15:11–32	A man with two sons is asked by the younger for his share of the family money. The son goes off and lives a riotous life until his money is exhausted. While working feeding pigs, he decides to go back and ask to be one his father's servants, since they were well cared for. His father sees him coming home while he is still far away and runs to him, kisses him, and treats him as an honored guest and son.	This parable challenges its audience to identify with the three main characters of the parable: The father, whose love allows him to move beyond his anger and disappointment and welcomes back his son; the older brother who, despite being a good son, is unable to move beyond his anger and welcome his once lost brother; and the younger son, who is able to move beyond his rebellion and pride and return to his father with humility and repentance. God, our Father, is compassionate and greatly rejoices when we return to him. God accepts all people, regardless of their past and actions, when they humbly come back to him with repentance.
34 *The Shrewd Steward* Luke 16:1–13	A steward is accused by his master of mishandling goods. The steward makes deals to reduce the amount owed by each of his master's debtors so that they will take care of him if he is dismissed.	This parable looks to what is wise living in light of the second coming. A wise person handles worldly wealth for the kingdom of God. No one can serve two masters: "God and Money" (Luke 16:13). The parable challenges us to use all of our resources to the service of the kingdom of God.
35 *The Rich Man and Lazarus* Luke 16:19–31	A rich man and a beggar (Lazarus) from his gates both die; Lazarus goes into Abraham's bosom (Paradise) and the rich man to torment in hell. The rich man asks Lazarus to bring him water (but he cannot pass) and to warn his brothers (but they would not believe).	This parable challenges its audience's notion of who has God's favor. Although the rich man felt confident that God was with him, God favored Lazarus. The problem with the rich man in the parable is not his wealth. Rather, the problem is wealth that ignores poverty and suffering.
36 *The Obedient Servant* Luke 17:7–10	A master expects a servant to perform his assigned duties. No additional reward is necessary.	Christians should not seek to be rewarded for their obedience. Rather, we should serve him out of love.

TITLE	SUMMARY	COMMENTS
37 *The Persistent Widow* Luke 18:1–8	A widow continuously pleads for justice from an uncaring judge. He grants her desire simply to spare himself her persistent requests.	The parable emphasizes God's patience toward his people, the assurance that God will act on their behalf, and the need to live with faithfulness and readiness for Jesus' return. The parable also shows the importance of persistence and perseverance. It is an invitation to ask God for what we need. It promises that a loving God is far more likely to respond positively to the perseverance of his people's requests than would an uncaring judge.
38 *The Pharisee and the Tax Collector* Luke 18:9–14	A Pharisee goes to the temple and prays boastfully about his works, how good he is, and how much better he is than the publican (tax collector). The tax collector humbly bows his head and asks God to forgive him of his sins.	This powerful, short parable makes an important implied conclusion: "righteous acts without compassion and love are not considered righteous by God."[1] It forces its audience to recognize that when we exclude anyone from God's grace, we run the risk of excluding ourselves from God. God honors and uplifts the humble but rejects the arrogant.
39 *The Ten Minas* Luke 19:11–27	Before traveling afar, a master gave each of his three servants ten minas (about three month's wages) to invest. One servant profited ten minas and another servant five. As a reward, the first was made ruler of ten cities, the second ruler over five. A third servant refused to invest the money because he feared his master; his mina was given to the servant who gained ten minas.	At his return, Christ expects Christians to have used the gifts and opportunities he has given them (Col.1:10). The central issue of the parable is faithfulness in the way we use the gifts God has given to us. The parable exhorts its audience to remain faithful disciples of Jesus in the time before his return.

Interpretation of Parables

Parables can be difficult to understand.

- One problem is the chronological and cultural gap between Jesus and us. The parables are expressed with objects and experiences of daily life: parenthood, seeds and grains, trees and animals. However, these are things not always accessible for people today.

- A great deal of the effectiveness of the parables lies in their evocative power. The parables remind people of their lives and important things in their lives. Parables in the Bible are effective because the original audiences "get them." Interpreting parables is like *getting* jokes; explaining a joke kills the joke. As modern readers, we may be too far removed from the original context to "get" the parables. Thus, we need to explain parables in such a way that we do not kill their effectiveness on today's audience.

- When we take the meaning of the Bible beyond what the Bible means, we often *allegorize*. Allegorization is the practice of turning into allegory what was *not* intended to be an allegory. An often-quoted example is Augustine's interpretation of the parable of the Good Samaritan. For Augustine, the man traveling represents Adam, Jerusalem is the heavenly city, Jericho stands for our mortality, the robbers are the devil and his angels, the priest and Levite are the priesthood and ministry of the Old Testament, the good Samaritan is Christ, the inn is the church, and so on. We can know whether a parable is an allegory if the Bible itself interprets it as an allegory. For example, in the parable of the Tenants in Matthew 21:33–45, the gospel writer suggests an allegorical parable. The audience of the parable understand that Jesus is referring to the prophets, which Jesus supports with his quote from Psalm 118. Although the landowner (God), the servants (the prophets), and the son (Jesus himself) do have an allegorical meaning, we should not extend the allegory to other elements of the story. The watchtower, for example, should not be allegorized, nor the journey. They are only support elements for the parable.

Following are general suggestions for interpreting parables. These suggestions are useful for understanding how parables work and what they mean. As an example, we read the parable of the lost sheep in Matt. 18:12–14 and Luke 15:4–7.

1. *Read the parable carefully and more than once. Read it in more than one translation.*
2. *Notice the structure of the parable.*
   - The structure of the text helps us discern what is important to the gospel writer. It helps us know where the main point is.
   - In the parable of the lost sheep, because Matthew emphasizes the action of seeking, the main point—the lost sheep—is right in the middle of the parable. Since Luke focuses on the joy that the finding causes, the main point of the parable is at the end.
   - Often, the main point of parables tends to be at the end of the story, but every parable must be interpreted on its own.
3. *Pay attention to the context of the parable.*
   - The evangelists present the parable to different audiences. In Matthew, Jesus tells the parable of the lost sheep to the disciples, whereas in Luke, Jesus speaks to the Pharisees.
   - Because the parables challenge listeners to do or change something, identifying the parable's audience is important in order to understand its meaning.
4. *Interpret what is given and not what is omitted.*
   - The fact that the shepherd leaves behind ninety-nine sheep should not prompt us to ask any "what ifs." Any dangers that the ninety-nine sheep may face are imaginary and not part of the parable. We must interpret only what is present in the parable.
   - The parable should not be used to define the salvation Jesus offers. The parable itself does not teach that God is a shepherd, though that is an image the Bible uses elsewhere.
   - Jesus' own interpretation of the parable makes it clear that the shepherd stands as a metaphor of God. However, we should not extend the metaphors and seek meaning for the hills or the one hundred sheep.

5. *Identify the main points and any secondary ones.*
   - The parable challenges its hearers to understand the value of all people, especially those who are lost.
   - It shows that just as a shepherd goes out of his way to find one lost animal and rejoices when he rescues his sheep, so does God rejoice when lost people are found by him.
   - Seeking the lost sheep and the joy of finding it are the main points of the parable.

6. *Detect the important cultural details in the parable that need explaining.*
   - The image of the shepherd was common in Jesus' times and instantly connected listeners with the Old Testament and the patriarchs.
   - But there's a twist: Shepherds were practical, and people assumed that a shepherd would not risk ninety-nine to save one. It is precisely this reversal of expectation that makes the parable so compelling. Sheep were valuable assets. Risking ninety-nine sheep for one is not a practical choice.
   - So Jesus used the expected to show something about God's character to bring his audience up short: God loves us so much he will risk everything for just one.

Characteristics of Jesus' Parables

Jesus' creative stories were:

- Brief
- Simple and repetitive
- Composed of items, examples, or experiences from his audience's daily experience

- Meant to have major and minor points
- Engaging for listeners at different levels
- Shocking, surprising, challenging, appealing, and relevant

- Often connected to the Old Testament and the kingdom of God

Function of Parables in Jesus' Ministry

Jesus' chief message was the arrival of God's kingdom to the world. Jesus' life, ministry, death, and resurrection bear witness to the reality and power of the kingdom. The parables also bear witness to this coming kingdom.

Although the parables were an important teaching tool for Jesus' ministry, their importance goes beyond instruction. Like the prophets of the Old Testament, Jesus used the parables as a way to confront people with God's word.

Parables are stories that demand a response. More than simply instructing, Jesus seeks from his audience a response to the coming of the kingdom. To do that, the parables are designed to provoke emotions, reactions, repentance, and recognition of who Jesus is and what the coming of the kingdom means.

The parables are an invitation to those who belong to God to strengthen their faith and knowledge. For those who have rejected God, the parables become confirmation of their unbelief. Like Isaiah before him, Jesus knew his message would present opposition, skepticism, and hostility. Because the parables appeal to our emotions and will, their message often produces a strong reaction in us.

Studying the Parables

Choose a parable to study. (You might want to start with The Pharisee and Tax Collector, The Good Samaritan, or The Rich Fool.) Study the parable by yourself or with a group.

Step one: Read the parable three times.

Step two: Examine the structure. How many parts does the parable have? Draw a simple outline of the parable.

Step three: Note the context. To whom is Jesus telling this parable? What is the setting? Did some event or question prompt Jesus to tell this parable?

Step four: Look up cultural and historical questions. When you read the parable, what questions about biblical culture or historical setting came to mind? (For example: What is a Pharisee? Who were the Samaritans? What did it mean for someone in Jesus' time to own large barns?) Write down your questions and look for answers using Bible dictionaries and commentaries.

Step five: Find the main point. What is the lesson to be learned for Jesus' audience? If a question or challenge prompted Jesus to tell the parable, how does this parable address that?

Step six: Consider how the parable can strengthen your faith and knowledge of God. Do you see similarities between the events or characters described in the parable and today's society or your own life? What does this parable teach you about God? What does it motivate you to do?

Endnote
Stories with Intent. K. R. Snodgrass. Eerdmans, 2008; p. 473

Contributing Authors: Benjamin Galan, MTS, ThM, Adjunct Professor of OT Hebrew and Literature at Fuller Seminary; Vincent Botticelli

Life of Joseph

God's Purposes in Suffering

Time Line • Family Tree • Map

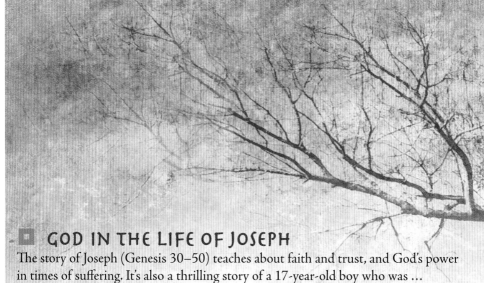

☐ GOD IN THE LIFE OF JOSEPH

The story of Joseph (Genesis 30–50) teaches about faith and trust, and God's power in times of suffering. It's also a thrilling story of a 17-year-old boy who was …

+ Favored by his father
+ Resented by his ten older brothers
+ Thrown into a pit in the wilderness
+ Sold into slavery and never returned home

Later — just when it appeared his life was improving —he was…

+ Stalked by someone powerful and vengeful
+ Falsely accused and imprisoned
+ Abandoned in jail without friends or supporters to defend him
+ Forgotten by people who owed him a favor

But throughout the misery, God was there with Joseph.

Joseph's story gives hope on four levels:

1. **Personal**: God has a purpose in our suffering. God grew Joseph from immaturity to strength and mercy.

2. **Family**: God used bad circumstances to save Joseph's family and change attitudes.

3. **Nationally**: God used Joseph's misfortunes to save many lives and set up the rest of the biblical story that leads to the saving of the world through Christ.

4. **Beyond**: God used this event to bring blessing to the world long past biblical days. We, too, are part of God's larger plan that calls for patience and trust during times of suffering, and will have results on this and the next generation.

◻ BEGINNING OF THE PROMISE (Gen. 12:1–3)

This story begins long before Joseph's birth. It begins with his great-grandfather, Abraham, a nomadic sheep and goat herder who lived in the dry, hot region of the Middle East known then as Canaan and today as Israel.

Although Joseph is the main character, the story is really about God's promise to Abraham's descendants.

> *God appeared to Abraham and made two promises:*
> • *I will make you a great nation.*
> • *All the nations of the earth will be blessed by you. (Gen. 12:1–2)*

God's promise to Abraham changed the direction of humanity. Human disobedience and rebellion turned God's creation upside down. Instead of being a good and blessed creation, human rebellion resulted in a cursed creation and a cursed history (see Gen. 1–3).

God promised Abraham to start a new history of blessing with him and his family.

God's promise lies with a family; it is not an ideal family—it resembles many families today, with struggles, deep problems, sadness, and grief.

Abraham's Departure by József Molnár

◻ A DYSFUNCTIONAL FAMILY

The story of Joseph begins in Gen. 37:1, with his father Jacob "in the land of Canaan." This simple statement is a reminder that God is implementing his promise to Abraham. Then the biblical story introduces Joseph and his brothers. It is immediately clear that their relationships are broken and that the potential for conflict is great.

◻ PLAYING FAVORITES

(Gen. 37:1–4)

Joseph is Jacob's youngest and favorite son.
This favoritism is evident in a few short lines in the story.

Two main clues of this favoritism:
1. The "coat of many colors," or "richly ornamented robe," was a gift from Jacob to Joseph. Whatever the robe was, it was a special and precious garment indicating that Joseph was not meant for a life of fieldwork like the other sons.

> The Bible describes a similar robe in only one other place, 2 Sam. 13:18. There Tamar, King David's daughter, wears a similar robe and we read, "for this was the kind of garment the virgin daughters of the king wore" (2 Sam. 13:18).

2. The other telling comment is of "a bad report" (see box) Joseph brings about his brothers. Jacob foolishly sends the favored son to check on his brothers. By this time, Joseph's actions and attitudes have hurt his relationship and angered his brothers.

◻ JOSEPH'S DREAM

(Gen. 37:5–11)

> The expression "**bad report**" is also used in Ps. 31:13, Jer. 20:10, and Ezek. 36:3, where it is used for the whispering of hostile people.

Joseph's ten older brothers resent their father's favoritism as much as Joseph's attitude. Young Joseph fails to understand the depth of his brothers' loathing toward him. With little tact and wisdom, Joseph shares his dreams with his family. One night, Joseph dreams that his brothers and parents bow before him. The Bible does not say that Joseph's dreams come from God. In fact, we do not know that is the case until the end of the story, when the dreams become reality. It is also the straw that breaks the camel's back for his brothers.

The Wages of Deceit

Jacob's relationship with his sons reflects a lifetime of deceit. Jacob deceived Isaac, his father, for his blessing—cheating his brother Esau out of a blessing that was rightfully Esau's. Jacob fled his brother's anger and traveled to Haran to live with his uncle Laban (Gen. 27). There, Jacob fell in love with Laban's youngest daughter, Rachel. However, Laban tricked Jacob into working seven years for his daughter, but he gave his oldest daughter, Leah, to Jacob in marriage. Jacob had to work another seven years for Rachel.

Jacob's love for Rachel was always greater than his love for Leah. However, God granted Leah many sons from Jacob, whereas Rachel was not able to give birth. Rachel finally bore a son to Jacob, Joseph (Gen. 29:31–30:24). Jacob's love for Joseph became an extension of his love for Rachel.

■ DECEIVING THE DECEIVER

(Gen. 37:12–36)

The strained relationships among family members anticipate a potentially tragic ending. Jacob sends Joseph to check on his brothers who are herding sheep far away—an unwise decision considering the previous "bad report" from Joseph and the already weak relationships among his children. Joseph's brothers find a perfect opportunity to be rid of their youngest brother. The brothers throw Joseph in a pit and want to kill him. Reuben hopes to rescue Joseph, but Judah, one of two eldest brothers, argues that it is better to make some money from the deal. Instead of killing him, they sell Joseph to a trading caravan going to Egypt. Joseph, although alive, ends up as a slave in Egypt. Jacob is cruelly deceived by his sons, who return with a bloodied coat/robe and a terrible lie: Joseph is dead.

The Promise in Danger

Can God's promise to Abraham (or any other promise) ever be in danger? Absolutely not. God is always faithful to his promises. However, in times of trouble, it is difficult to remember this truth and easy to assume the worst. No, the promise is not in danger; though Joseph might find it difficult to believe while being dragged away from his family and into slavery. As readers, we can do nothing but weep along with Jacob: weep for Jacob's pain, for Joseph's fate, and for the brothers' hardness.

◻ A STORY WITHIN A STORY (Gen. 38)

Right in the middle of the story of Joseph, the Bible pauses and tells a separate story.

Joseph's brother Judah, now a grown man with three sons, tries to deceive his daughter-in-law, Tamar, by promising to follow the biblical laws that will protect her but actually refusing to carry them out. As time goes by, Tamar realizes she has been denied her proper rights; she turns around and deceives Judah.

Judah and Tamar by Horace Vernet

In a family with a history of lying and violence, betrayal and hatred, how did God change Judah's heart? Judah had to admit that his actions had been wrong—far worse than his daughter-in-law's. He admitted that Tamar was more righteous than he was. Judah, a man unable to regret his mistreatment of his brother Joseph and his father, who lies and does injustice to his daughter-in-law, is a changed man. He is finally able to confess his error and make things right for Tamar.

While Joseph is in Egypt, God starts the change in Joseph's brothers.

◻ FROM POWERLESS TO POTIPHAR'S (Gen. 39:1–6)

Joseph goes from being the beloved son to being sold as a powerless slave in a powerful Egyptian officer's home. Potiphar is the captain of Pharaoh's bodyguard. In spite of this terrible reversal of fortunes, Scripture tells us, "The Lord was with Joseph." We do not know if Joseph, the shepherd boy, knew the language. It is unlikely that he was educated at the level of Egyptian upper class, but the Bible is clear that Joseph does not give up. He works hard and contributes to Potiphar's household. Every small responsibility he handles is successful. Over time, Potiphar realizes that the Lord is with this slave, and Potiphar puts Joseph in charge of everything he owns.

■ REJECTION AND REVENGE (Gen. 39:7–19)

Potiphar's wife wants Joseph to sleep with her, but Joseph refuses, calling her proposed actions
  ◆ a breach of his responsibilities
  ◆ a betrayal of Potiphar who has trusted him
  ◆ a sin against God

She will not take no for an answer, so she stalks him. Day after day she talks with him, trying to seduce him. But one day, they are in the house alone and she grabs his clothing. Her grip must have been strong, because to get away he had to shed that garment and run outside. This final rejection leads her to revenge. She calls out to the men in the household and claims she has been attacked. When Potiphar hears, he is angry and throws Joseph in jail.

■ FROM POTIPHAR'S TO PRISON (Gen. 39:20–23)

Joseph is not given a trial; he is unfairly thrown into a jail for the king's prisoners. Scripture says he was there for many years. It was another reversal of fortunes. A good man treated wrongly, framed, betrayed by his employer's wife despite his flawless performance.

No one would blame Joseph for becoming angry and bitter, but he didn't. However, "the LORD was with Joseph" (Gen. 39:2). Joseph used his administrative skills to help, and over time was put in charge of all the prisoners and the prison organization. He found favor with the chief jailer, whose confidence in Joseph was so high that he didn't even supervise Joseph.

Joseph and Potiphar's Wife
by Guido Reni

◻ MORE HOPES DASHED (Gen. 40)

Two new prisoners from Pharaoh's household were placed in the jail for offending their master. Joseph was put in charge of them and took care of them for a long time. One night both men had troubling dreams, and in the morning Joseph noticed they were sad because there was no one to explain the dreams to them. Joseph told them that interpretations of dreams belonged to God and if they told him, he would explain it.

◻ THE CUPBEARER AND BAKER'S DREAM

	Dream	Interpretation from God
Cupbearer	A vine with three branches producing grapes. Grapes were squeezed and the juice given to Pharaoh.	In three days Pharaoh will give you back your job.
Baker	Carrying three baskets of bread for Pharaoh on his head. Birds came and ate them.	In three days Pharaoh will have you executed.

Interesting points:
- Joseph noticed that the men were troubled in the morning and asked about it. He who had been insensitive to his brothers' feelings now cared about others.
- Joseph gave credit to God rather than to himself, despite having a reputation as a clever man.
- Joseph asked the cupbearer to remember him and asked for help to get him out of jail.

Within three days both predictions come true. The cupbearer is restored to his place of privilege and the baker is executed. But the cupbearer forgets about Joseph, and Joseph continues to live in a dungeon several more years.

© Catalin Petolea

■ PHARAOH'S DREAM (Gen. 41:1–36)

One night Pharaoh has two dreams that none of his magicians and wise men can interpret.

Dream 1	Seven cows come out of the Nile River. They are sleek and fat and grazing. Seven more cows come out of the Nile. These are ugly and gaunt. They eat the sleek fat cows.
Dream 2	Seven ears of plump good grain appear on one single stalk. Then seven thin and scorched ears sprout up and swallow the plump ears.

Suddenly the cupbearer remembers Joseph and tells about the Hebrew slave who interpreted his own dream two years before. Pharaoh calls for Joseph. Joseph has to shave and change clothes from his prison garb. Pharaoh says, "I have heard it said about you, that when you hear a dream you can interpret it." Joseph replied, "It is not in me; God will give Pharaoh a favorable answer."

When Joseph hears the dreams, he calls them parallels having the same message.

Interpretation

After seven years of abundance in the land of Egypt, seven years of famine will ravage the land. The double dream means that God will surely do this and do it soon.

Recommendation

Pharaoh should find a wise supervisor to put in charge. Then appoint overseers who will collect and store one fifth of the annual food harvests in Egypt for the seven good years. This reserve will keep the people of Egypt from perishing.

Of Dreams and Gods

Dreams were important in the ancient world, especially in Egypt. The Egyptians had texts that priests would use to interpret dreams. Dreams were windows into the world of the gods. For this reason, priests were the people who could best interpret them.

When Pharaoh asks Joseph to interpret his dreams, Joseph replies, "I cannot do it, but God will give Pharaoh the answer he desires" (Gen. 41:16). Joseph claims that his God, the God of the Bible, can do something Pharaoh's gods have failed to do. Joseph is confident because, as he said before, "Do not interpretations belong to God?" (Gen. 40:8). It is an astonishing claim. Although the Egyptians were quite open to other people's gods, they were confident their own gods were superior. Joseph's claim suggests that the interpretation of dreams belongs to God because revelation through dreams comes from God! Joseph is proclaiming God's superiority over the Egyptians gods.

◼ WHAT A DIFFERENCE A DAY MAKES

(Gen. 41:37–57)

Pharaoh sets Joseph over all Egypt, gives him his signet ring of authority, clothes him in fine linen and emblems of power, and puts him in a chariot and makes him his second-in-command.

For 13 years, Joseph has been a slave in Egypt and now he is second in command, and given every honor of status and fame and a notable marriage. At age 30, he is given the responsibility to travel through Egypt and supervise the storage of grain in locations owned by Pharaoh. He is so successful and the abundance is so great that even he can no longer keep track of the massive amounts of harvest.

◼ JOSEPH'S BROTHERS IN EGYPT (Gen. 42:1–44:34)

Part of God's promise to Abraham finds fulfillment through Joseph here. However, another important part of God's promise was that Abraham's descendants would make a great nation. This part of the promise implies a people and a land. The story is not over, the promise is still incomplete.

Just then, Joseph's brothers arrive in Egypt on a mission to save their family from starvation. This surprise encounter sparks a series of events that transforms Joseph and his brothers' lives forever.

As his brothers arrive and bow down to the Egyptian lord, Joseph recognizes his brothers, but they do not recognize him. The statement reminds the readers of the brothers asking their father to *recognize* (the Hebrew word means *recognize*, "examine" in the NIV) Joseph's bloodied garment (Gen. 37:32).

This recognition brings Joseph's memories back like a flood. As his son Manasseh's name reminds us, Joseph had been able to forget his difficult past (see Gen. 41:51; Manasseh probably means "to forget"). Now, the memories, the pain, the anger, and the doubts arise with renewed impetus.

Joseph Accuses His Brothers

Joseph speaks harshly to the brothers and accuses them of being spies. This is not a light issue; the brothers understand immediately that they are in mortal peril. The Egyptian lord does not have to offer proofs for his accusation and could execute them at any moment with a simple command. Sheer terror makes them tell the truth about themselves: "We are all the sons of one man. Your servants are honest men, not spies." Their claim is another way to say they have clan responsibilities.

Joseph tests their claim of being honest men and accuses them again of being spies. The brothers insist, "Your servants were twelve brothers, the sons of one man, who lives in the land of Canaan. The youngest is now with our father, and one is no more" (Gen. 42:13). Joseph learns more about his family—his father is still alive and there is a new member of the family, Benjamin.

In this brief episode we can imagine a divided Joseph: a man full of anger and overwhelmed with memories but also full of wisdom and responsibility. Joseph is a changed man. However, if Joseph is changed, have his brothers changed at all? Are they still the same foolish men, willing to destroy a person's life to quench their anger?

Joseph Tests His Brothers

Joseph tests his brothers more than once, first by hiding his true identity, then by making them leave Simeon as a guarantee that they would return with their youngest brother. The brothers fail to persuade their father to let them bring Benjamin with them to Egypt. Jacob, a broken man, bitterly reminds them of Joseph—Jacob refuses to trust them with Benjamin's life for he fears the ending will be as tragic as that of Joseph's. Reuben makes a proposal: the lives of his two children for the life of Benjamin. Jacob has already lost two children (Joseph and Simeon). Why would he risk losing Benjamin and two grandchildren? Reuben's proposal is reckless. Jacob decides not to send Benjamin with them.

Since the famine is so severe, Jacob's sons need to return to Egypt. Judah steps forward and makes a wise suggestion. If something happens to Benjamin, Judah accepts the guilt and responsibility himself. It is a wise and mature proposal. In the ancient world, a verbal promise was not a thing lightly taken. Verbal commitments were a guarantee of action. Because of Judah's promise, Jacob reluctantly accepts; the twelve brothers are on their way back to Egypt.

Joseph continues the charade. He knows his brothers will return for his brother Simeon; but would they do the same for Benjamin?

Through yet another test, Joseph forces his brothers to demonstrate the kind of men they have become. When Benjamin is falsely found guilty of stealing a silver cup, Joseph quickly and angrily issues the punishment: Benjamin is to remain as his slave. But Judah steps up and demonstrates his moral quality and maturity. He explains to Joseph his own promise to Jacob. He says, "Now then, please, let your servant remain here as my lord's slave in place of the boy, and let the boy return with his brothers" (Gen. 44:33).

Judah has changed; he is no longer the self-centered man who once chose personal gain over his brother's safety, and personal security over his daughter-in-law's righteous claim.

▪ RECONCILIATION IN EGYPT (Gen. 45:1–50:26)

Joseph cannot control himself and reveals his identity. While Joseph is moved to tears, his brothers are terrified when they finally recognize him. Joseph makes the wise and powerful statement: "But God sent me ahead of you to preserve for you a remnant on earth and to save your lives by a great deliverance. So then, it was not you who sent me here, but God" (Gen. 45:7–8). Joseph and Pharaoh invite Jacob and everyone in his family to come to Egypt.

Before leaving Canaan, the land God had promised to Abraham, Jacob has a dream. In the dream, God tells him, "I am God, the God of your father.... Do not be afraid to go down to Egypt, for I will make you into a great nation there. I will go down to Egypt with you, and I will surely bring you back again" (Gen. 46:3–4). God is renewing his promise to Abraham. God will make Abraham's descendants into a great nation *in* Egypt. Then, God will give this new nation a land where God will dwell with them.

Years later, after Jacob's death, Joseph's brothers still wonder if now Joseph will take revenge against them. Instead, Joseph says, "Don't be afraid. Am I in the place of God? You intended to harm me, but God intended it for good to accomplish what is now being done, the saving of many lives" (Gen. 50:19–20).

© Galyna Andrushko

◼ THE GOD WHO WAS THERE

Through Joseph's life, we can learn how God moves in the lives of his people. Throughout the story, we find God at crucial moments. He is not always acting directly, but his presence is constant, causing or enabling all possible movement: geographic, moral, from foolishness to wisdom. Through the movement in Joseph's story, God redeems a broken family.

Joseph	• Joseph moved from Canaan to Egypt. • He moved from being a spoiled, foolish young man to being a wise man. • He moved from anger and forgetfulness to forgiveness and restoration. • He is redeemed from his sufferings in Egypt. • He is redeemed from being the victim of violence and injustice from his brothers. • He is redeemed from his own anger and memories. • He is redeemed by learning wisdom and trusting in God.
Jacob	• Jacob moved from being the deceiver to being deceived. • He moved from the joy of his favorite son to the tragedy of his supposed death. • He moved from being a man defeated to being a man with a future. • He is redeemed by receiving God's renewed promise. • Though he had become a broken man, God's gracious acts through Joseph allow Jacob to have a renewed sense of hope for the future. • This hope includes the promises that God made to Abraham.
Joseph's Brothers	• They moved from their wicked deeds to willingness to accept their responsibility. • They are redeemed from their early, evil ways.
Judah	• Judah moved from being a man merely concerned with his own well-being to one willing to accept the consequences of his actions. • Later, when Jacob blesses his children, Judah receives this blessing: "The scepter will not depart from Judah, nor the ruler's staff from between his feet" (Gen. 49:10). • From Judah, King David would be born, and, later, Jesus, the promised Messiah, the one who fulfilled God's promises. • Judah is redeemed from his previous egotism. • He becomes the leader of the children of Israel. • Through him, the Messiah is born.

Although this story does not explain every case of suffering and grief, it instructs us on how to acquire the necessary wisdom that will allow us to face such experiences. The Bible recognizes that doctrinal statements are not enough to deal with suffering and grief. Wisdom allows us to see life from God's perspective.

When we can see life through wisdom, we can trust that God will allow "neither death nor life, neither angels nor demons, neither the present nor the future, nor any powers, neither height nor depth, nor anything else in all creation, will be able to separate us from the love of God that is in Christ Jesus our Lord" (Rom. 8:38–39) and that "all things God works for the good of those who love him…" (Rom. 8:28).

Life of Joseph

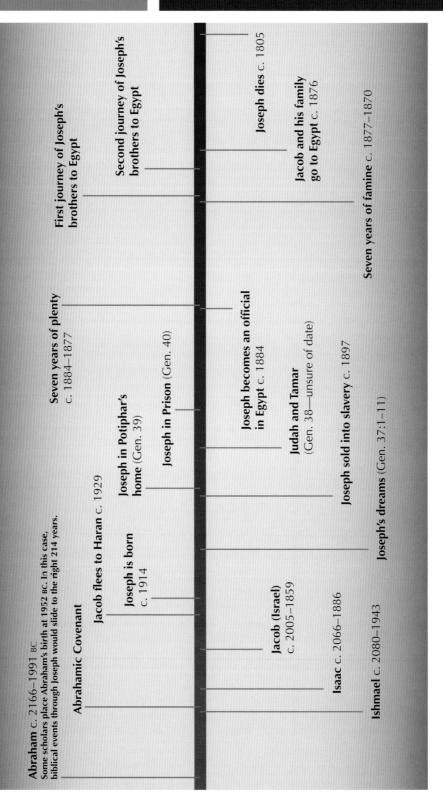

Abraham c. 2166–1991 BC
Some scholars place Abraham's birth at 1952 BC. In this case, biblical events through Joseph would slide to the right 214 years.

Abrahamic Covenant

Jacob flees to Haran c. 1929

Seven years of plenty c. 1884–1877

First journey of Joseph's brothers to Egypt

Second journey of Joseph's brothers to Egypt

Joseph dies c. 1805

Joseph in Potiphar's home (Gen. 39)

Joseph in Prison (Gen. 40)

Joseph becomes an official in Egypt c. 1884

Jacob and his family go to Egypt c. 1876

Joseph is born c. 1914

Judah and Tamar (Gen. 38—unsure of date)

Joseph sold into slavery c. 1897

Seven years of famine c. 1877–1870

Jacob (Israel) c. 2005–1859

Joseph's dreams (Gen. 37:1–11)

Isaac c. 2066–1886

Ishmael c. 2080–1943

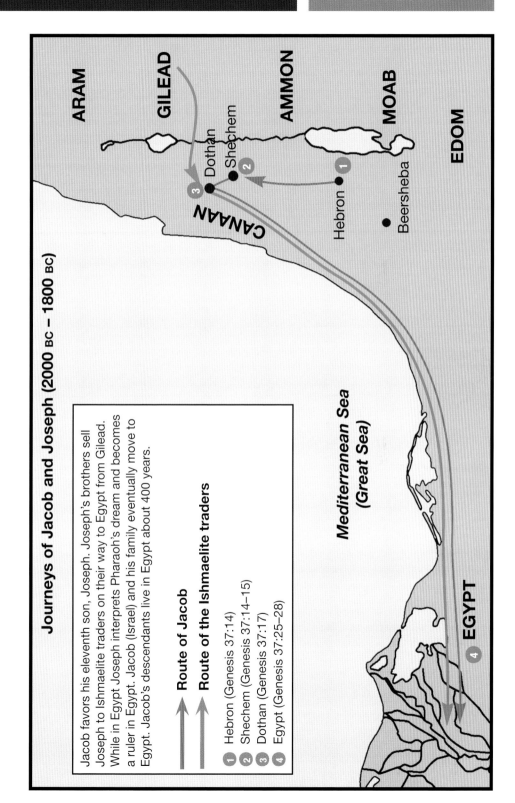

Journeys of Jacob and Joseph (2000 BC – 1800 BC)

Jacob favors his eleventh son, Joseph. Joseph's brothers sell Joseph to Ishmaelite traders on their way to Egypt from Gilead. While in Egypt Joseph interprets Pharaoh's dream and becomes a ruler in Egypt. Jacob (Israel) and his family eventually move to Egypt. Jacob's descendants live in Egypt about 400 years.

Route of Jacob

Route of the Ishmaelite traders

1. Hebron (Genesis 37:14)
2. Shechem (Genesis 37:14–15)
3. Dothan (Genesis 37:17)
4. Egypt (Genesis 37:25–28)

ARAM

GILEAD

AMMON

MOAB

EDOM

CANAAN

Dothan

Shechem

Hebron

Beersheba

Mediterranean Sea (Great Sea)

EGYPT

Joseph's Family Tree

The story of Joseph is part of the larger story of how God fulfilled his promise to Joseph's great-grandfather, Abraham. Just like his father had done, Jacob blessed his children before dying (the brief sentence below summarizes Jacob's blessings to each of his children in Gen. 49:1–27). The traditional list of Israel's twelve tribes includes Joseph's sons, Ephraim and Manasseh, but not Joseph. Jacob adopted Joseph's sons as his own children (Gen. 48:5–20). By doing this, Jacob exalted Joseph to his own level as a patriarch of the Tribes of Israel, and granted his children a sharing in the promises God made to Abraham. (Because Levi's descendants became the priestly tribe, they did not partake in the distribution of the promised land. Thus, they are not counted in the twelve tribes of Israel.)

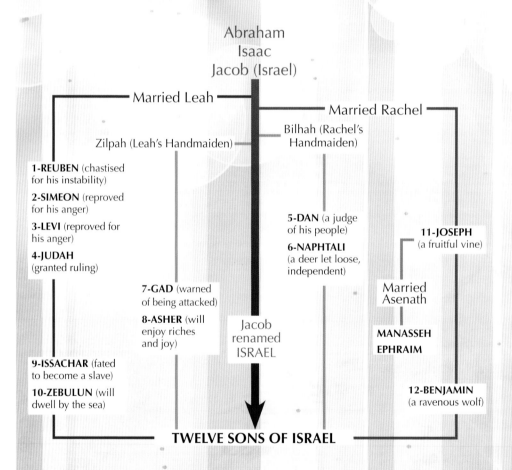

Abraham
Isaac
Jacob (Israel)

Married Leah — Married Rachel

Zilpah (Leah's Handmaiden) — Bilhah (Rachel's Handmaiden)

1-REUBEN (chastised for his instability)

2-SIMEON (reproved for his anger)

3-LEVI (reproved for his anger)

4-JUDAH (granted ruling)

5-DAN (a judge of his people)

6-NAPHTALI (a deer let loose, independent)

11-JOSEPH (a fruitful vine)

7-GAD (warned of being attacked)

8-ASHER (will enjoy riches and joy)

Jacob renamed ISRAEL

Married Asenath

9-ISSACHAR (fated to become a slave)

10-ZEBULUN (will dwell by the sea)

MANASSEH
EPHRAIM

12-BENJAMIN (a ravenous wolf)

TWELVE SONS OF ISRAEL

Author: Benjamin Galan, MTS, ThM, Adjunct Professor of OT Hebrew and Literature at Fuller Seminary.

Esther

Courage for Dangerous Times
Biblical Insights
Historical Background

CHOSEN FOR SUCH A TIME AS THIS

When the opposition seems unbeatable, does God care? Am I alone in this world, with its suffering, injustice, and pain? Where can I go to resign when life becomes too tough? How can I risk my reputation, comfort, and future to rescue others?

These are questions that come up in the life of Esther.

It's easy to dismiss Queen Esther as a lucky young woman who won the heart of the king. But realistically, she was a woman with a tragic background and dangerous secret that could cost her life and her family's. She was married to a king who destroyed peoples' lives on a whim and had a history of killing people close to him. Worse still, the king's favorite counselor and chief advisor was a mortal enemy of Esther's family. Esther had to keep a low profile, keeping her secret, hoping he wouldn't make the connection.

For Esther, life was unfair. But her story brings hope to all who face trouble by showing how God works even through the fears and dangers.

Character	Genealogy	Actions in History
King Ahasuerus (Xerxes)	Persian king Son of Darius I of the royal Persian line	The king in the Book of Esther Invaded Greece, but later defeated by Greece Assassinated by courtiers
Queen Vashti	Queen of King Xerxes May be Amestris, daughter of Otanes	Loses her position as queen for disobeying the king's orders
Mordecai	Son of Jair (Esther 2:5) of the first royal line of Israel (Kish/Saul 1 Sam. 9:1)	Raised his cousin Esther Prevents the assassination of the king Becomes the king's main advisor
Esther	Mordecai's cousin	Lost both of her parents; raised by her cousin. Wins over the king to become queen in a dangerous time Saves the Jewish people from genocide
Haman	Born of the royal line of the Amalekites (line of King Agag) an important detail.	King's main advisor Plots the destruction of all the Jews in the Persian Empire Is hung on the gallows

THE MISSING CHARACTER

Yet the missing character in the book of Esther is the one who has the largest role: God, conspicuous by his absence, who uses the actions of the human characters to shape all of history.

• God worked through the Persian king's own weaknesses to preserve the Jewish people.

• God worked through the courage of Mordecai and Esther to keep the Jewish people from harm and redeem a family name (1 Samuel 9:1; 15).

• God overturned Haman's evil plans, and fulfilled a 500-year-old prophecy of judgment on the Amalekites (Haman's ancestors) (1 Samuel 15:1–3).

POMP IN THE PERSIAN PALACE

This story takes place in the Persian royal court in Susa—a world of power where decisions, obsessions, and whims of the people with power in this world affect thousands. The book of Esther presents a childish, whimsical, unpredictable, and dangerous King Xerxes who acts in a drunken stupor, thoughtlessly punishes his own queen, is easily swayed by advisers around him, and is a danger to his people. However, these very qualities generate not only the main crisis in the book, but also its solution.

The book opens with Queen Vashti refusing to obey the king who wants to parade his beautiful wife in front of his banquet guests. On the urging of his advisors, the king deposes Vashti, leaving himself without a queen. Vashti's act of defiance sets up a series of events that will include conspiracy, pride, lies, murderous plots, unexpected heroism, and deliverance. A beleaguered, young Jewish woman is placed in a position of power and responsibility. The future of her people, endangered by a vindictive and ancient enemy of God's people, Haman, the Agagite, is in her hands. But, where is God in all of this? Are the Jews in Persia, and in many other places of the ancient world, all alone?

SUSA

Susa (Shushan in the Old Testament) is an ancient city in Iran today. Some of the oldest written records referenced this city. As Empires appeared and disappeared, Susa became Akkadian, Babylonian, Assyrian, Persian, Macedonian, Parthian, Roman, and Muslim.

In the 6th century BC, King Cyrus' son, Cambyses II, transferred the capital of the Persian government from Pasargadae to Susa. His son, Darius I (Xerxes' father), extended and improved a road from Susa to Asia Minor in the West and to East to India. This road was known as the "Royal Road." The road was crucial for Imperial communication and commerce. Several centuries later the Royal Road became part of the "Silk Road" that joined the West to India and China.

PERSIA

Persia became the dominant power of the ancient world in the 6th century BC. Under the leadership of Cyrus the Great, the Persian Empire (also known as the Achaemenid Empire) conquered Babylon in 539 BC. Besides being a brilliant warrior and conqueror, Cyrus was also a great politician. He created a policy to send people previously conquered in Babylonian and Assyrian times back to their homelands.

The Bible portrays Cyrus as God's instrument to free and restore the Jews to the Promised Land (Ezra 1:1–6, 6:1–5; Isaiah 44:23–45:8; 2 Chronicles 36:22–23). Thus, a group of Jews returned to Jerusalem to rebuild the walls and the temple around 515 BC. Other Jews, like Mordecai and Esther, remained in Persia.

The Persians remained in power until 330 BC when Alexander the Great, the Macedonian conqueror, defeated the armies of Darius III and occupied Persepolis, the capital of the Persian Empire.

KING XERXES (486-465 BC)

• Called Ahasuerus in the Bible

• Known for his war against the Greeks: Despite his famous loss at the Battle of Thermopylae in 480 BC (the basis for the famed Leonidas of Sparta and his 300 warriors), Xerxes led his armies to sack Athens.

• A year later, however, the Greeks expelled the Persian army from the Greek islands to Asia Minor.

• Much of the information about this war comes from the accounts of the historian Herodotus.

The "Cyrus Cylinder" proclaims Cyrus as the legitimate king of Babylon. It also describes how Cyrus won the respect and favor of the Babylonian priests when he restored the temples in Babylon.

© Arvel Witte

ONE QUEEN, TWO IDENTITIES

After Vashti is stripped of her crown, the king finds a new queen: a young, beautiful woman whose identity seems irrelevant at the time. Her name is Esther. On Mordecai's instructions, Esther hides her Jewish identity and successfully blends into the Persian culture. The king is so pleased with his new queen that he throws a great banquet in her honor and proclaims a holiday throughout all the provinces.

What's In A Name?

The books of Daniel and Esther both depict life for Jews in exile. They show that Jews in prominent places had both Hebrew and Babylonian names.

Hebrew Name	Meaning	Alternate Name	Meaning
Daniel	God is my judge	Belteshazzar	Bel protect his life. (Bel is another name for Marduk.)
Hadassah	Myrtle	Esther	Star
(No Jewish name mentioned)		Mordecai	Related to the Babylonian chief god Marduk

Why Were the Jews in Persia?

In 722 BC the powerful king of Assyria, Sargon II, conquered and destroyed Samaria. Almost two hundred years later, Nebuchadnezzar, king of Babylon, conquered the kingdom of Judah.

From 597 BC through 586 BC, Nebuchadnezzar systematically undermined Judah until he destroyed Jerusalem and its temple.

To avoid rebellion and exert complete dominance, both Assyria and Babylonia deported people. By uprooting people from their land and their gods, they were easier to control. Some of the Jews who were taken from their homes during these years went to Persia.

God's presence in the Jerusalem temple was a direct source of assurance and security for the Israelites, God's chosen people. If God was with them and dwelt among them, who could dare challenge them? However, the Babylonians not only conquered them but also destroyed their temple. Because every region had its own local gods, wars were also representations of divine wars. In conquering Judah, the Babylonians could claim that their god, Marduk, was superior to the Jewish God, Yahweh—a tremendous spiritual blow to the Jews (see for example 2 Kings 18:31–35).

Exiled Jews not only lost their homes and their land, but also the certainty of God's presence. In light of this desperation and spiritual grief, the words of the prophet Isaiah echo powerfully: "Comfort, comfort my people, says your God" (Isaiah 40:1).

When King Cyrus allowed the Jews to return to Jerusalem about 70 years later, an event Isaiah prophesied as God's own action (Isaiah 44:28–45:13), many who had already begun a new life in exile stayed in Babylon and Persia.

Beauty Secrets

Everything we know about Esther's personality is derived from her actions and the responses of people around her. The expression "won his favor" (2:9, 15) is a clue to Esther's personality. The common expression is for someone to "find favor" with a king. However, Esther "won" the king's favor, showing Esther as active and purposeful. She is no passive and powerless observer in this story; rather, she shows herself to be daring, intelligent, and strong despite having been orphaned in her youth.

But before Esther won the king's favor, she won the favor of the man in charge of all the virgins. Hegai "quickly" provided Esther with the diet and beauty treatments required, and even advanced her to the best spot in the harem! Clearly, Esther showed pleasing qualities that wore well with those who mattered. But the depth of her ability to choose wisely and to trust worthy advice is shown in her willingness to rely on Hegai's advice as to what to bring with her when it was Esther's turn to go in to the king. And the payoff is big—the king is so pleased that he crowns Esther as his new queen.

In the dangerous atmosphere of the Persian court, where conspiracies were thick and executions routine, Esther's apparent serenity stands out. She "won the favor of everyone who saw her." Her life must have seemed charmed—until the royal shoe dropped.

Intrigue in the Persian Court

Esther's cousin Mordecai, a Jew from the tribe of Benjamin, holds a high post at the royal residence. Mordecai overhears two guards plotting to kill the king, which he reports to Queen Esther who exposes the plot. The Bible relays this event without giving it much importance, but it turns out to be crucial in the climax of the story. Not only does the event determine Mordecai's future, it shows the intolerant reaction that the king has to betrayal and deception—he hangs the two guards on gallows.

Because of Mordecai's position of high visibility in the royal residence, Haman, an Amalekite and the king's closest advisor, notices Mordecai. Haman is a vain and conceited man and the mortal enemy of the Jews. Haman determines that everyone should treat him as royalty. However, Mordecai refuses to bow down before him. Haman persuades the king to approve an edict he has written to annihilate all the Jews—men, women, and children—in every province of Persia.

Why did Mordecai Refuse to Bow?

The text does not specify the reasons for Mordecai's refusal.

Possible reasons:

- Mordecai's religious conviction that only God deserves praise, or

- A reflection of the ancient enmity between the Amalekites and Israelites. Mordecai's refusal provides the excuse for Haman's hatred and homicidal plans.

An Ancient Feud

The Amalekites were semi-nomadic people, descendants of Esau (Genesis 36:11–12).

They became one of Israel's most bitter enemies.

They made an unexpected attack against Israel at Sinai (Exodus 17:8–16).

King Saul's failure to destroy the Amalekites, especially their King Agag, was one of the main reasons God eventually rejected Saul as king of Israel (1 Samuel 15).

The enmity between the descendants of Agag and Saul, Amalekites and Benjaminites, became an essential part of Esther's story in the Persian court.

Haman was Agag's descendant (Esther 3:1).

Mordecai was a Benjaminite (Esther 2:5).

A Queen's Courage

When Haman's plan for the Jews' destruction becomes public, Mordecai laments, and the Jews join him. Mordecai turns to Queen Esther to save the Jews by pleading with the king. Mordecai gives this message to Esther: "And who knows but that you have come to royal position for such a time as this."

Esther requests that Mordecai and the Jews join her in a three-day fast, after which she submits to whatever is to happen: "I will go to the king, even though it is against the law. And if I perish, I perish" (Esther 4:14, 16). Esther's memorable words are born from faith and fear. She is afraid of the unpredictable nature of the king who could legally have her executed for approaching him without being called. She has faith that someone above the powerful king himself is in control. In either case, these words show Esther's courage and willingness to risk her life for her people.

Esther relied on this courage for the next crucial steps. After days of severe fasting (and the implied accompanying prayer) Esther approaches the king, but instead of anger from this unpredictable man, she is met with hiss favor.

Just as this whole story begins at a banquet, Esther plans to appeal to the king at a banquet. Unexpectedly, Esther does not express her request to the king at the first banquet. Instead, she asks him and Haman to return for a second banquet.

Fasting Turns to Feasting

The repetition of Esther's banquets parallels the king's banquets earlier in the story.

The King's Banquets	Esther's Banquets
The king calls Queen Vashti to the banquet, but she refuses to come.	Esther invites the king and Haman to a banquet; they agree to go.
The king becomes furious and listens to bad advice.	The king is pleased and generous toward Esther.
The king rejects Vashti as his queen.	The king confirms Esther as his queen by his willingness to grant her any favor. Esther invites the king and Haman to a second banquet.
Esther wins the king's favor to become queen.	Having the king's favor, Esther reveals her request and Jewish identity to the king. The king becomes furious and condemns Haman.
As a celebration, the king gives a great banquet in honor of Esther.	Queen Esther and her people are thus saved from Haman's evil plans. They celebrate with feasting and establish the Feast of Purim to commemorate the event.

Royal Humiliation

Between Esther's two banquets, another important event takes place. Haman's wife and friends advise him to build gallows and ask the king to hang Mordecai on them. Haman is so prideful and confident of his success that he builds the gallows, but Haman is doomed.

Meanwhile, back at the palace, the king has insomnia. To help him sleep, the king orders the chronicles of his reign to be read to him. By apparent coincidence, the chronicles contain the record of Mordecai exposing the plot to kill the king. When the king is reminded of this event, he wishes to follow tradition by rewarding the hero. Instead of deciding on his own how to reward Mordecai, the indecisive king looks around for someone to ask how to do this. Although Haman is actually approaching the king to request the execution of Mordecai, the king requests Haman's advice on how to honor a hero! In an ironic reversal Haman is bitterly humiliated when the king orders him to follow his own advice and honor Mordecai as a hero!

Haman returns home to receive a harsh warning from his wife and advisors: "Since Mordecai, before whom your downfall has started, is of Jewish origin, you cannot stand against him" (Esther 6:13). Before Haman can respond, the king's officers hurry him off to Esther's second banquet.

Such a reversal of fortune is an illustration of this prayer in the Bible: "He raises the poor from the dust and lifts the needy from the ash heap; he seats them with princes and has them inherit a throne of honor" (1 Samuel 2:8).

Character	Traits	Life Lessons
King Xerxes	Foolish, rash, and acts in fits of anger	"A wise man fears the Lord and shuns evil, but a fool is hotheaded and reckless" (Proverbs 14:16). "Everyone should be quick to listen, slow to speak and slow to become angry, for a man's anger does not bring about the righteous life that God desires" (James 1:19–20).
Esther	Humble, faithful, and courageous even though fearful	"The Lord preserves the faithful, but the proud he pays back in full. Be strong and take heart, all you who hope in the Lord" (Psalm 31:23–24). "Humble yourselves before the Lord and he will lift you up" (James 4:10).
Haman	Prideful and arrogant	"Pride goes before destruction, a haughty spirit before a fall" (Proverbs 16:18). "There is no wisdom, no insight, no plan that can succeed against the Lord" (Proverbs 21:30).
Mordecai	Dedicated, and was used as an instrument of justice	"The Lord works righteousness and justice for all the oppressed" (Psalm 103:6). "Rescue the weak and needy; deliver them from the hand of the wicked" (Psalm 82:4).

IRONY AND DESPAIR

At Esther's second banquet, she chooses to express her request. When Esther reveals her Jewish identity and Haman's plot to destroy her and her people, the king's anger is not surprising. Haman realizes his doom at once.

The king leaves the room in a fit of rage. In the meantime, Haman realizes his only chance to escape alive. He falls over Esther in despair, seeking her favor. Haman had wanted all to bow down to him, now Haman is begging for his life. Haman's wife had already anticipated this "falling" (Esther 6:13). As this happens, the king enters the room.

The king accuses Haman of attempting to molest Esther. How could the king misunderstand Haman's intentions? Did he need a further reason to condemn him? This scene is parallel to the conspiracy Mordecai discovered earlier in chapter 2. There, the king made sure the information was correct before condemning the guards who had conspired against him. Here, Haman falling over the queen gives King Xerxes the perfect excuse to avoid investigation. In the ancient world, taking a king's wife or concubine was a claim to the throne (for example, that is what Absalom did with David's concubines in 2 Samuel 16:21–22). In another "coincidence," one of the servants happens to remember that Haman had built an enormous gallows to hang Mordecai. Ironically, Haman is hung on those very gallows.

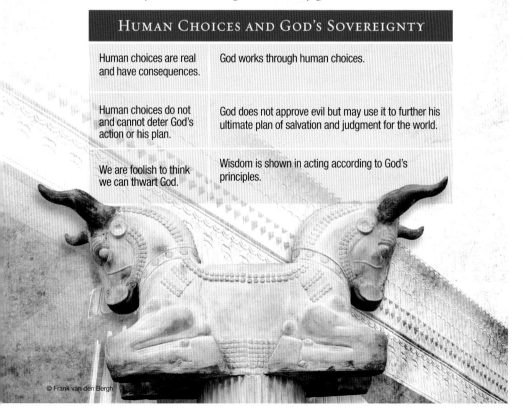

HUMAN CHOICES AND GOD'S SOVEREIGNTY

Human choices are real and have consequences.	God works through human choices.
Human choices do not and cannot deter God's action or his plan.	God does not approve evil but may use it to further his ultimate plan of salvation and judgment for the world.
We are foolish to think we can thwart God.	Wisdom is shown in acting according to God's principles.

© Frank van den Bergh

ONE MORE REQUEST

Although the king's fury subsides after Haman's hanging (7:10), the original decree to destroy the Jews is still in force. Esther requests one more favor of the king. The request is similar to Haman's own request in chapter 3. The king's response is equally indifferent in both cases: he leaves the writing of the decree to someone else. Since "no document written in the king's name and sealed with his ring can be revoked" (8:8), the king allows Mordecai and Esther to write another edict to spare the Jews from destruction. Mordecai receives the king's signet ring, which grants him the same status that Haman previously enjoyed. Mordecai and Esther write the edict in the name of the king sealed with the signet ring. The narratives of the writing and communication of both edicts are parallel.

Each edict produces a reaction from the city of Susa—the Persian capital—and the Jewish people. In the first edict, "the city of Susa was bewildered" (3:15) and "there was great mourning among the Jews" (4:3). But upon news of the second edict, "the city of Susa held a joyous celebration" and for the Jews it was a time of "happiness and joy, gladness and honor" (8:15–16).

Chapter 9 commemorates the salvation of the exiled Jews in the Persian Empire. It recognizes the reversal of fortunes (9:1). The Jews moved from lament and mourning to rejoicing and celebration: "I will turn their mourning into gladness; I will give them comfort and joy instead of sorrow" (Jeremiah 31:13). This event became an annual festival, similar to the Passover. Although God saved his people on many occasions, only a few are remembered with festivals.

Important historical and cultural events in the 5th century BC (499–400 BC)		
APPROX. DATE	ISRAEL/MESOPOTAMIA	GREECE/EGYPT/CHINA
500–450 BC	Judah continues in exile in Babylon and Persia. The first group of exiled Jews returns to Jerusalem with Ezra and Nehemiah (around 458 BC). Around 486 BC, Xerxes I of Persia makes Esther his queen. Xerxes I is assassinated in 465 BC. Persia continues its expansion to the West and faces the Greeks.	Confucius teaches throughout China around 495 BC. Egypt is under Persian rule. The Battle of Thermopylae between the Persians and the Spartan King Leonidas occurs in 480 BC. After the Greeks defeat the Persians, the First Peloponnesian War begins between Athens and Sparta in 457 BC. Lives of Pericles, Athenian politician; Sophocles, Euripides, Aristophanes, Greek dramatists; Herodotus, historian; Hippocrates, physician; Anaxagoras and Socrates, philosophers.
449–400 BC	This is where the Bible ends its history of Israel. Persia administers the land of Israel.	The Second Peloponnesian War begins in 431 BC. Sparta defeats Athens in 404 BC.

REVERSAL OF FORTUNE

The great reversal in Susa is still remembered in the feast of Purim, which is celebrated between February and March. The word Purim comes from a Hebrew word meaning "lot" (*pur*). Ironically, Haman used the word first. Haman chose the date when the Jews would be destroyed by casting a lot (something like dice). On the very date that Haman had planned for the destruction of the Jews he lost his life, showing that coincidence does not exist, but God is in control of what happens. "The lot is cast into the lap, but its every decision is from the LORD" (Proverbs 16:33).

The story ends with a brief epilogue highlighting Mordecai's position in Persia. It reassures the reader that the Jews were safe and prosperous even in this distant land.

PURIM CELEBRATIONS TODAY

Purim today is a minor festival which many Jews no longer celebrate. For those who do celebrate it as a religious holiday, it is a joyous celebration of God's grace and liberation, with parties, food, and gifts. During the service at the synagogue, as the story of Esther is read, and people hiss and boo every time Haman's name is mentioned and cheer when Mordecai's name is mentioned. There are four main traditions people observe for Purim:

- listening to a reading of the Book of Esther,
- giving of gifts—usually food, pastries, or other sweets,
- giving charity to the poor as a way to express gratitude to God,
- eating a special meal in community to celebrate God's saving actions.

One of the special foods for this festival is a pastry called *hamantaschen*. They are triangle-shaped cookies filled with fruit (prune, dates, apricot) or a mixture of poppy seeds. In some traditions, the name *hamantaschen* refers to Haman's hat (or ears) which fell when he was executed.

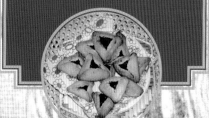

God's Presence and Absence

An important question arises when reading the book of Esther: Where is God in this story? The name of God or any explicit reference to him is missing. The apparent absence of God is more than an oversight. It is a theological point, one that is expressed through the literary medium. The Jews in exile had to answer crucial questions about themselves: Were they still part of God's people? Could they lay claim to God's promises to Abraham? Was God with them? In the past, God had manifested himself with power in miracles of salvation and liberation. Would God also act there in Persia, away from the land God had promised Abraham?

The book provides a series of events when things first fell apart and then came together. For the person of faith, those who know God's actions in history, God is present and active in the story. As shown above, there are different ways the writer reminds readers of God's actions: subtle references to Exodus, Joseph, and the Judges. One of the best clues, however, is Esther herself.

Throughout biblical history, God chooses the least likely person. The stories in the book of Judges show God choosing unlikely heroes: Ehud, Deborah and Jael, Gideon, and so on. Esther is a heroine because she acted in unexpected ways for her people. She surpassed everyone's expectations. Although the text does not explicitly state that her actions were born of faith, her obedient and courageous attitude, her willingness to follow Mordecai's advice to help the Jews, and her own wise choices demonstrate a person who knew how God acted in history. Esther stands in contrast to King Xerxes who in weakness relied on bad advice; Mordecai stands in contrast with Haman who devilishly offered bad advice.

God's presence and his behind-the-scenes activity are also known as "divine providence," that is, God's continuous care for his creation. As the exiled Jews wondered about God's presence, the Scriptures show that his presence and care were there all along. God fulfilled his promise to Abraham: "I will make you into a great nation, and I will bless you; I will make your name great, and you will be a blessing. I will bless those who bless you, and whoever curses you I will curse; and all peoples on earth will be blessed through you" (Genesis 12:2–3).

THE GREATEST REVERSAL

Although the reversal of fortunes in Esther was extraordinary, it was not the greatest reversal God has prepared. The greatest reversal came in the most unexpected way: in a humble king who was born in a barn, who rode a donkey, who lived with the poor, ate with tax collectors, became a friend to prostitutes, and died a humiliating death on the cross. In Jesus Christ, God produced the greatest reversal of history since creation itself. He is creating a new people, changing lives, and using humble, Esther-like people to bring about even more reversals. God defeated an arrogant, evil enemy who thought himself victorious. And one day this great reversal will end with a wonderful climax: a new heaven and a new earth (Revelation 21:1). In that day, God "will wipe every tear from their eyes. There will be no more death or mourning or crying or pain, for the old order of things has passed away" (Revelation 21:4).

Although God is never truly absent (for the Spirit is always present), often in moments of grief and suffering one feels as if God were far away. At the moment of greatest need and suffering on the cross, Jesus lamented God's absence (Matthew 27:46). Jesus, in his full humanity, also experienced and suffered God's apparent absence.

The book of Esther is a reassurance, not only for the Jews in exile, but also for Christians who "are still in the world … but are not of the world" (John 17:11, 15). An assurance that even when God seems to be absent from our world or suffering, he is ever present, interested, and ready to act. The book of Esther affirms in narrative form what the Apostle Paul affirmed in his letter to the Romans:

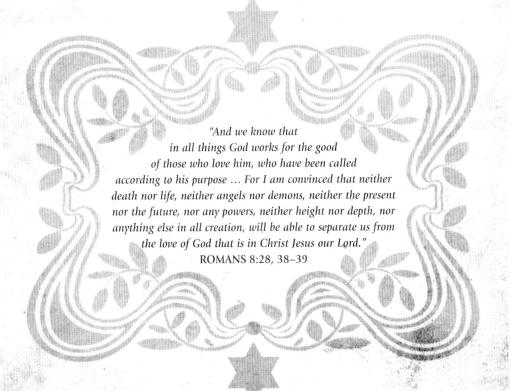

"And we know that in all things God works for the good of those who love him, who have been called according to his purpose … For I am convinced that neither death nor life, neither angels nor demons, neither the present nor the future, nor any powers, neither height nor depth, nor anything else in all creation, will be able to separate us from the love of God that is in Christ Jesus our Lord."
ROMANS 8:28, 38–39

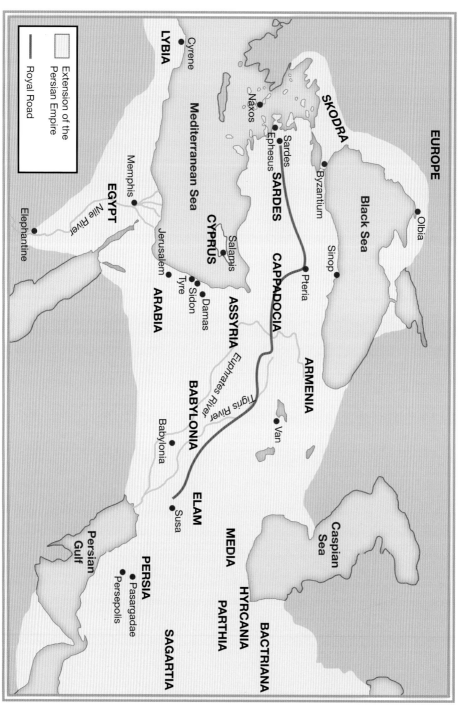

PERSIAN EMPIRE

Author: Benjamin Galan, MTS, ThM, Adjunct
Professor of OT Hebrew and Literature at Fuller Seminary.

Proverbs

My son, if you will receive my words and treasure my commandments within you, make your ear attentive to wisdom, incline your heart to understanding;

The wicked earns deceptive wages, but he who sows righteousness gets a true reward.

Biblical Wisdom for Today

How to Read Proverbs

Proverbs: A Guide to Godly Living

"An apple a day keeps the doctor away..." We all have heard or used some of these pithy sayings at one point or another. They express popular wisdom about the world that anyone can understand and apply. Their content expresses an observation about nature or society or advice concerning behavior or making choices.

People understand that following the advice of these wise sayings will help one to live a better life. Part of their effectiveness lies in their brevity—they are easy to remember. These sayings are most effective when we quote them at the right moment and in the right circumstances.

> Proverbs are short, memorable sayings that generalize on human experience to communicate an experiential truth.

Although we all recognize that these bits of wisdom are helpful, they are not universal or always applicable. While generally "an apple a day keeps the doctor away," we all know that some serious illnesses require immediate medical attention. In other words, we all recognize the limits of popular wisdom.

In the following pages, we will learn about biblical proverbs from the book of Proverbs: their background, hints and steps for interpretations, main themes, and connections with the New Testament and the church today.

wisdom

Wisdom is often defined as "the ability to make godly choices." In the Bible, wisdom is tightly connected to creation. The way God created the universe has a direct effect on the way nature and society behave. In an important sense, wisdom is the ability to see life and the world the way God sees them. Wisdom is practical knowledge that allows people to live fully.

proverb

Proverb is a short, memorable saying that communicates an observation of the world or experience that helps one live better. The Hebrew word behind it is *mashal*. Among its meanings are: to rule and to compare or liken. The wisdom of proverbs helps wise people to master the art of godly living, as well as to discern how our lives and our behavior are connected with God's creation.

Who Wrote the Book?

- Proverbs 1:1, 10:1, and 25:1 affirm that King Solomon, King David's son, was the main author.
- Proverbs 25:1 also affirms that "the men of Hezekiah king of Judah" copied them.
- The book also recognizes other contributors: Wise men (22:17; 24:23), Agur (30:1), and Lemuel (31:1). Nothing is known about these writers.
- We read in 1 Kings 4:32 that Solomon wrote three thousand proverbs.

fear of the Lord

The Bible is clear that "the fear of the Lord is the beginning of knowledge" (1:7). In the Bible, the starting point of wisdom and its end-goal are an all-embracing relationship with God, the LORD of the covenant. The fear of the LORD is not a sense of terror but of reverence. In other words, it is a deep sense of who God is and who we are in relation to him. It is a deep understanding that God is the creator, sustainer, savior, judge, and owner of the whole universe. This knowledge is a relational knowledge that affects our behavior. The psalmist explains, "The Lord delights in those who fear him, who put their hope in his unfailing love" (Ps. 147:11). Fearing the LORD, then, takes the form of trust: trust in God's faithfulness to his promises as creator, redeemer, savior, and judge.

How Is the Book Arranged?

The structure of the book gives us an overview of the content and themes. The main sections of the book of Proverbs are:

1. Introduction to the book (1:1–7)
2. Instructions and warnings (1:8–9:18)
3. First collection of Solomon's proverbs (10:1–22:16)
4. First collection of the words of the wise (22:17–24:22)
5. Second collection of the words of the wise (24:23–34)
6. Second collection of Solomon's proverbs (25:1–29:27)
7. The words of Agur (30)
8. The words of Lemuel (31:1–9)
9. Poem of the virtuous woman (31:10–31)

Wisdom Literature

As "an apple a day" illustrates, proverbs do not occur exclusively in the Bible. The book of Proverbs is an example of a wider category of wisdom literature. In ancient Egypt and Mesopotamia, wisdom played an important role. In those societies, wisdom belonged to the royal court. Wise teachers instructed their royal students for important positions within the kingdom. From scribes to nobles, wisdom taught the proper— wise—behavior in the court, correct speech, and an understanding of society and the world that allowed them to serve the ruler effectively.

Wisdom Literature in the Bible

The book of Proverbs is an example of a wider category of wisdom books in the Old Testament.

Wisdom Books	Wisdom Themes in Other Books
• Job • Proverbs • Ecclesiastes	• Song of Songs • Psalms (for example, 1, 19, 34, 49, 78, 119) • Genesis (1–2, 37–50) • Amos and Isaiah • Daniel

Biblical wisdom literature shares themes, vocabulary, and genres with this international wisdom tradition. However, there are important differences between the wisdom of the Bible and that of the world around ancient Israel. Some are shown below.

	Egypt and Mesopotamia	Old Testament
Focus	Anthropocentric (man-centered) The main interest was on finding ways for people to be successful in life. Material success was emphasized.	Theocentric (God-centered) The main focus is on the God who created with order. Success in life is connected to human relationship with God.
God	Since these societies were polytheistic, their wisdom depended on a personal god or a number of other gods. Each god provided some wisdom.	The Bible declares over and over than only the Lord is God, and he alone. God is the source of all wisdom because he himself created wisdom and he created *with* wisdom.
Audience	The main audience for wisdom teachers were court officials and royalty.	Wisdom is meant for all people. Although the emphasis in Proverbs is on "sons," the other wisdom books make it clear that wisdom is for all.
Goal	Help civil servants to be effective and successful in their work and life in general.	Teach people to love wisdom by having a correct relationship with God, by understanding the order with which God created the universe, and by recognizing the limits of human wisdom.

Main Themes in the Book of Proverbs

Wisdom We can read the whole book as an appeal to choose wisdom over all other things.

God created wisdom (8:22–23)	*The Lord brought me forth as the first of his works, before his deeds of old; I was appointed from eternity, from the beginning, before the world began.*
God used wisdom to create the universe (8:24–31)	*Then I was the craftsman at his side. I was filled with delight day after day, rejoicing always in his presence.*
God reveals and is the source of wisdom (2:6–7; 30:5–6)	*For the Lord gives wisdom, and from his mouth come knowledge and understanding (2:6–7).*
The beginning of wisdom is "fear of the Lord" (1:7; 2:5; 9:10; 10:27; 14:27; 15:16, 33; 16:6; 19:23; 22:4; 23:17)	*The fear of the Lord is the beginning of knowledge, but fools despise wisdom and discipline (1:7).*
Wisdom is desirable over all things (4:7–9; 8:10–11)	*Choose my instruction instead of silver, knowledge rather than choice gold, for wisdom is more precious than rubies, and nothing you desire can compare with her (8:10–11).*

Understanding Humanity Wisdom teaching is directed to all people. Proverbs is an invitation to accurately identify the source of all wisdom, neither over- nor underestimating human wisdom. In the book of Proverbs we learn about humans:

Humans are God's creation (29:13)	*The poor man and the oppressor have this in common: The Lord gives sight to the eyes of both.*
Humans delude themselves (12:15; 14:12; 16:2; 25; 28:26)	*There is a way that seems right to a man, but in the end it leads to death.*
The heart is central and reveals humanity's true character (27:19)	*As water reflects a face, so a man's heart reflects the man.*
Humans are inherently foolish (22:15)	*Folly is bound up in the heart of a child, but the rod of discipline will drive it far from him.*

Description of a wise person

Wisdom is not something easily taught. As with many important things, it is easier to *show* what a wise person looks like than describe wisdom. Wise people are recognized by their:

Character	
They are righteous (13:5–6; 12:17)	*The righteous hate what is false, but the wicked bring shame and disgrace. Righteousness guards the man of integrity, but wickedness overthrows the sinner (13:5–6).*
Loyal (16:6)	*Through love and faithfulness sin is atoned for; through the fear of the LORD a man avoids evil.*
Humble (3:5, 9; 8:17; 28:13; 21:4)	*He who conceals his sins does not prosper, but whoever confesses and renounces them finds mercy (28:13).*
Teachable (12:1, 15; 3:1; 10:14; 15:12; 17:10; 18:15)	*The heart of the discerning acquires knowledge; the ears of the wise seek it out (18:15).*
Self-controlled and not rash (17:27; 14:29, 30; 19:2)	*A man of knowledge uses words with restraint, and a man of understanding is even-tempered (17:27).*
Forgiving (10:12; 17:9; 14:9; 20:22; 24:29)	*Do not say, "I'll do to him as he has done to me; I'll pay that man back for what he did" (24:29).*
Thoughtful (13:16; 14:8, 15, 16; 22:5)	*A simple man believes anything, but a prudent man gives thought to his steps. A wise man fears the LORD and shuns evil, but a fool is hotheaded and reckless (14:15–16).*
Is honest (12:22)	*The LORD detests lying lips, but he delights in men who are truthful.*
Does not boast (27:2)	*Let another praise you, and not your own mouth; someone else, and not your own lips.*
Does not reveal secrets (17:9; 20:19)	*He who covers over an offense promotes love, but whoever repeats the matter separates close friends (17:9).*
Does not slander (6:12)	*A scoundrel and villain, who goes about with a corrupt mouth.*
Is peaceful (12:16)	*A fool shows his annoyance at once, but a prudent man overlooks an insult.*

Speech

Words have power (10:11; 12:18)	*Reckless words pierce like a sword, but the tongue of the wise brings healing (12:18).*
Limits of words (14:23; 28:24; 26:18–19)	*Like a madman shooting firebrands or deadly arrows is a man who deceives his neighbor and says, "I was only joking!" (26:18–19).*

Relationship with Wife

He recognizes she is from God (18:22; 19:14)	*Houses and wealth are inherited from parents, but a prudent wife is from the LORD (19:14).*
Acknowledges as his crowning glory (12:4; 31:28)	*He who finds a wife finds what is good and receives favor from the LORD (12:4).*
Is faithful to her (5:15–20; 6:29)	*Drink water from your own cistern, running water from your own well. Should your springs overflow in the streets, your streams of water in the public squares? Let them be yours alone, never to be shared with strangers. May your fountain be blessed, and may you rejoice in the wife of your youth (5:15–18).*

Relationships with Children

Acknowledges the need for wisdom in their lives (1–9)	*My son, do not forget my teaching, but keep my commands in your heart, for they will prolong your life many years and bring you prosperity (3:1–2).*
Recognizes children's natural condition (22:15)	*Folly is bound up in the heart of a child, but the rod of discipline will drive it far from him.*
Children can be trained (19:18; 22:6)	*Train a child in the way he should go, and when he is old he will not turn from it (22:6).*
Recognizes that foolish children are in danger and wisdom can help (20:20	*If a man curses his father or mother, his lamp will be snuffed out in pitch darkness.*
Loves children and disciplines them (13:24)	*He who spares the rod hates his son, but he who loves him is careful to discipline him.*

Relationships with Other People

Chooses kind friends (22:24–25)	*Do not make friends with a hot-tempered man, do not associate with one easily angered, or you may learn his ways and get yourself ensnared.*

Values and is loyal to friends (27:10; 17:17) 	*Do not forsake your friend and the friend of your father, and do not go to your brother's house when disaster strikes you—better a neighbor nearby than a brother far away (27:10).*
Behaves fairly and justly with all (3:27–28)	*Do not withhold good from those who deserve it, when it is in your power to act. Do not say to your neighbor, "Come back later; I'll give it tomorrow"—when you now have it with you.*
Is considerate (25:17)	*Seldom set foot in your neighbor's house— too much of you, and he will hate you.*
Lives in peace (3:29; 25:8–9)	*Do not plot harm against your neighbor, who lives trustfully near you (3:29).*

Possessions

Recognizes the proper value of money (30:7–9; 11:4)	*Wealth is worthless in the day of wrath, but righteousness delivers from death (11:4).*
Wisdom is better than riches (15:16; 16:8, 16; 22:1)	*How much better to get wisdom than gold, to choose understanding rather than silver! (16:16).*
Honors God with possessions and recognizes that blessings come from God (3:9–10; 10:22; 14:24)	*Honor the Lord with your wealth, with the firstfruits of all your crops; then your barns will be filled to overflowing, and your vats will brim over with new wine (3:9–10).*
Recognizes that foolish behavior leads to poverty (6:6–11; 10:4–5; 21:17; 26:13–15), as do injustice and oppression (13:23; 16:8; 22:16)	*He who loves pleasure will become poor; whoever loves wine and oil will never be rich (21:17). He who oppresses the poor to increase his wealth and he who gives gifts to the rich— both come to poverty (22:16).*

A good man leaves an inheritance for his children's children, but a sinner's wealth is stored up for the righteous.

Is generous with possessions (3:27–28; 11:24; 28:27; 29:7)	*The righteous care about justice for the poor, but the wicked have no such concern (29:7).*
Is kind to animals (12:10)	*A righteous man cares for the needs of his animal, but the kindest acts of the wicked are cruel.*

Kingship In the world of ancient Israel, the King represented the people. Kings were meant to model attitudes, behaviors, and character that all people should display in their lives. Jesus, the King of kings, plays this role when he shows us what it means to be God's children. Thus, the king should:

Know his place (21:1)	The king's heart is in the hand of the Lord; he directs it like a watercourse wherever he pleases.
Be wise (8:15–16)	By me kings reign and rulers make laws that are just; by me princes govern, and all nobles who rule on earth.
Be righteous (25:5)	Remove the wicked from the king's presence, and his throne will be established through righteousness.
Be just (28:8; 29:4, 14)	If a king judges the poor with fairness, his throne will always be secure (29:14).
Have self-control (31:1–7)	[D]o not spend your strength on women, your vigor on those who ruin kings. "It is not for kings, O Lemuel—not for kings to drink wine, not for rulers to crave beer (31:3–4).
Be compassionate (31:8–9)	"Speak up for those who cannot speak for themselves, for the rights of all who are destitute. Speak up and judge fairly; defend the rights of the poor and needy."
Be surrounded by godly people (16:13; 22:11)	He who loves a pure heart and whose speech is gracious will have the king for his friend (22:11).

genre Genre refers to the sorting of written texts into categories. Separating texts in genres is helpful for understanding the ways different texts work internally, as well as the settings in which they were used. For example, we have different expectations from a letter from a bank than we do a letter from a loved one. Each type of letter produces certain expectations and prompts a specific response.

The Bible contains different genres: narrative, prophecy, poetry, wisdom, apocalyptic literature, gospel, letters, history, and others. Each general genre is subdivided into smaller types. Wisdom, for example, is subdivided into proverbs, instructions, speeches, and advice. Knowing the genre helps us know the intention for the text.

Parallelism

Parallel lines are an important feature of biblical proverbs. English proverbs normally have one line—"a penny saved is a penny earned." Hebrew proverbs normally have two lines—"A fool finds pleasure in evil conduct, but a man of understanding delights in wisdom" (10:23).

The sense of the proverb is found in the interplay of these lines.

Parallelism means that the second line of the verse advances the thought of the first line in some way. Determining how this movement occurs allows us to understand the sense and meaning of the proverb. There are different kinds of parallelism; the following examples are the most common types of parallelism in the book of Proverbs.

Kings take pleasure in honest lips; they value a man who speaks the truth (16:13).	In this example, we find these parallels: 1. Kings are the main subject of the whole verse. 2. *Taking pleasure* is parallel to *value*. However, valuing something is a step beyond merely taking pleasure. 3. *Honest lips* is parallel to *a man who speaks the truth*. Although both expressions mean the same, the second one further specifies what honest lips are. 4. Some call this type of parallelism *synonymous parallelism*.
A fool finds pleasure in evil conduct, but a man of understanding delights in wisdom (10:23).	1. This verse presents a contrast which provides the parallelism. 2. *A fool* is contrasted with *a man of understanding*. 3. Another parallel is the action of each person: one *finds pleasure* whereas the other *delights*. The two concepts are closely related, though the first one seems more impulsive. 4. The true contrast is on what each one finds delight in: the fool finds pleasure in *evil conduct*, while the man of understanding delights in *wisdom*. 5. The final contrast is the key to the verse. Like the rest of Proverbs, the book invites its readers to delight in wisdom. Some call this contrasting parallel *antithetical parallelism*.
Better a meal of vegetables where there is love than a fattened calf with hatred (15:17)	1. Another important form of parallelism is often called "better than" proverbs. 2. These proverbs explain why wisdom is superior to folly. 3. In the book of Proverbs, riches can be a blessing from God. But not all riches are desirable. When riches are accompanied by hatred, then poverty with love is preferable.

Lady Wisdom and Lady Folly

The function of the book of Proverbs is to persuade and instruct. First, the book invites readers to make a decision. The choice is not only a rational one; it involves desires and emotions, as well as intelligence and discernment. The writer attempts to capture the reader's will by appealing to the imagination.

Although the book addresses men only, as was traditional in ancient societies, its lessons are meant for all of God's people.

In the first nine chapters, the book addresses a "son." For young men, the choice of the right woman is life changing. Proverbs invites its readers to make an equally life-changing choice. Choosing wisdom over folly changes people's lives in a powerful way.

Wisdom and Folly are characterized as women. The readers "hear" from both Lady Wisdom and Lady Folly. Their invitations become alternatives between life and death. When reading the book of Proverbs, we must allow it to touch our emotions and our wills. We must allow ourselves not just to choose Lady Wisdom but also to love and pursue her.

Proverbs in Context

Although we can read each proverb separately, biblical proverbs were placed, by divine will, in a specific book context. The book of Proverbs is also part of a larger conversation with the other "wisdom books" of the Bible. Proverbs, Job, and Ecclesiastes balance and complement each other's views about wisdom, God, creation, humanity, and every important topic of the Bible.

A superficial reading of the book of Proverbs could suggest that the world functions with a perfect retribution theology: good things happen to good people, and bad things happen to bad people. As tempting as that might be to believe, the story in the book of Job calls us to be cautious. While Job's three friends argue individually that God rewards the righteous and punishes the wicked, Job continues to defend his own innocence. As readers, we know from the introduction in chapters one and two that Job is being used and abused by Satan, with God's authorization.

Job pleads for an audience with the creator. When he gets one, Job does not receive answers but a series of questions from God. God shows that he alone is wise; Job humbly recognizes the limits of his own wisdom, and declares, "Surely I spoke of things I did not understand, things too wonderful for me to know...My ears had heard of you but now my eyes have seen you. Therefore I despise myself and repent in dust and ashes" (Job 42:3, 5–6). At the end, God justifies and restores Job. He also rebukes Job's friends for their foolishness.

Just as the book of Proverbs is an invitation to fall in love with Lady Wisdom, the book of Job is a reminder that we should not fall in love with our own wisdom.

Proverbs Today

Should we read the Proverbs today? Yes! And not only should we read them, but we need to allow the beauty and desirability of Lady Wisdom to captivate our imaginations and wills. The consequences of our efforts will be evident in:

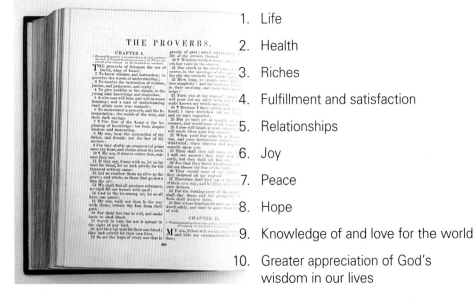

1. Life

2. Health

3. Riches

4. Fulfillment and satisfaction

5. Relationships

6. Joy

7. Peace

8. Hope

9. Knowledge of and love for the world

10. Greater appreciation of God's wisdom in our lives

We will also be able to know and relate better to Jesus, "who has become for us wisdom from God..." (1 Cor. 1:30). In Jesus, God reveals the extent, depth, and power of his wisdom.

Reading Proverbs

Since the wisdom in the book of Proverbs is important for our lives today, how can we study them profitably? Below are common mistakes we make when reading the book and some suggestions for studying Proverbs.

Common mistakes when reading Proverbs

1. *Ignoring the genre of the book.* Biblical proverbs are not promises, nor are they universal, timeless truths. Although there are wonderful truths to learn from them, and some clarification on doctrinal matters, the role of the proverbs is to challenge our minds, hearts, and wills.

2. *Isolating individual proverbs from the rest of the book and Bible.* If we read only, "Lazy hands make a man poor, but diligent hands bring wealth" (Proverbs 10:4), we would get the impression that laziness is the cause for poverty. However, the book of Proverbs also makes it clear that other reasons exist. "He who oppresses the poor to increase his wealth and he who gives gifts to the rich—both come to poverty" (Proverbs 22:16,) suggests that oppression and lack of opportunities are also causes of poverty.

3. *Forgetting the limits of wisdom.* The most evident limit is that proverbs are not adequate for every occasion. Reading and applying the sayings of the book requires wisdom: "Like a thornbush in a drunkard's hand is a proverb in the mouth of a fool" (26:9) and "A man finds joy in giving an apt reply—and how good is a timely word" (15:23). The wisdom of the proverbs are limited by their genre and good timing for their use. Also, although the proverbs reveal some of God's wisdom, our wisdom to understand and apply it is limited. Knowing that Jesus is the fullness of God's wisdom is a reminder that the wisdom we find in the book of Proverbs is limited.

Suggestions for reading the book of Proverbs

1. Remember that the meaning of individual proverbs is determined by the whole book's message.

2. Be sensitive to the metaphors and other literary devices in the book. Be especially attentive to the parallelism of lines.

3. Discern the specific message of the proverb. Then identify the contexts in which that particular proverb is applicable. Not all proverbs are applicable to all occasions. Part of what it means to be a wise person is knowing when and how wisdom is applicable.

4. Use commentaries to help you interpret cultural or literary issues. Proverbs uses imagery and customs that require knowledge of the ancient world.

5. If studying a theme in the book of Proverbs, like riches or discipline, read the entire book of Proverbs in more than one translation. Make notes of verses or sections that relate to the theme you are interested in. Then gather all the relevant verses and organize them in a way that makes the theme clear and does justice to the overall theme and message of the book of Proverbs.

6. The proverbs call us not to simply gain more knowledge but to become wiser in our doings and sayings. Search for a person who might be a good illustration of the wisdom you are studying. Remember that Jesus is the best illustration of God's wisdom.

"Whoever gives heed to instruction prospers, and blessed is he who trusts in the LORD." —Proverbs 16:20

Author: Benjamin Galan, MTS, ThM, Adjunct Professor of OT Hebrew and Literature at Fuller Seminary.

CHAPTER 5

Life of David

God's Power in Flawed People

Time Line • Map • Family Tree

Foreshadowing of the Messiah

A Man After God's Own Heart

King David's humanity is a clear and compelling to any reader. Modern readers, centuries after his time, can still relate to his story. The Bible presents a realistic picture of a man who loved God, became a great instrument in God's plans, and was deeply flawed. David is a person we can easily relate to.

Although David's victories are exciting and stir our imaginations, David's failures and humility are what make him a powerful character and his life so meaningful. David's life shows that human weakness is the perfect opportunity for God's grace, power, strength, forgiveness, justice and holiness to shine incomparably.

Samuel—Last of the Judges

In order to understand David's role in the story of Israel, we must see him in contrast to Israel's previous leaders.

- Forty years before David, Samuel was the last of the judges who brought order and unity as God's priest and prophet.
- Samuel symbolized God's own willingness to hear his people— *Samuel* means "God has heard."
- The people asked him to give them a king , an act that seemed to show disrespect for the Lord.
- He was hesitant, but God directed him to grant their request.
- He anointed Israel's first king, Saul—the name *Saul* means, "The one who was requested."
- Later he brought God's judgment against Saul when Saul rebelled against the Lord.
- He anointed David to be king instead of Saul.

"We want a king over us. Then we will be like all the other nations, with a king to lead us and to go out before us and fight our battles." When Samuel heard all that the people said, he repeated it before the Lord. *The* Lord *answered, "Listen to them and give them a king."* —1 Sam. 8:19–22

The Judges

When God brought Israel out of Egypt, Israel was not a nation yet. It was, rather, a group of tribes. When they arrived in the Promised Land, the land was distributed among the Israelites. At that point, each tribe governed itself separately. When a crisis arose, God would choose special leaders to fight in favor of God's people. They received a special calling; often God's Spirit empowered them in special ways to carry on a special task.

The Prophet Samuel fresco painting.

SAUL, FIRST (AND FAILED) KING OF ISRAEL

- Saul was "without equal among the Israelites…" (1 Samuel 9:2).
- Under his leadership, the Philistine threat was weakened but not eliminated.
- Saul was reluctant to become king. After Samuel anointed him, Saul returned to his regular activities (1 Sam. 11:5).
- Saul led Israel's armies to battle to save the city of Jabesh (1 Sam. 11).
- After an impressive victory, the people of Israel accepted Saul as their king.
- Saul made bad decisions that threatened his own kingship.

Why was Asking for a King a Bad Idea?

- The Tribes of Israel were without a king because God himself was their King. He governed them through the Law (Torah, the first five books of the Bible) and through the leadership of chosen people: judges, priests, prophets at crucial times.
- Israel was a chosen nation. God chose Israel to be his own treasured possession (Ex. 19:5). Israel should not have been like the nations around them (this is the theme of the whole book of Deuteronomy; see, for example, chapters 7 and 8).
- One of the purposes of the Law (Torah) was to help Israel be different from the peoples who lived around them (Deut. 7).

Saul Attacking David by Guercino

CALL OF DAVID—THE SINGING SHEPHERD

- God rejected Saul because of his rebelliousness.
- God sent Samuel to anoint the new chosen king of Israel.
- When Samuel visited David's father Jesse, Samuel expected the new king to be like Saul: impressive and imposing. Yet, God led the prophet to the last son: a small, young shepherd boy.
- After Samuel anointed him, David went back to his sheep.
- Although God had rejected Saul and anointed David as the new king, Saul continued to be king for sometime— perhaps for another 15 years or so.
- During that time, David came to be part of the royal court as a musician.
- David's music helped Saul find relief from his anguish.

Israel's Singer of Songs

David was called "Israel's singer of songs." David was gifted artistically as well as with weaponry. Among the many Psalms that are attributed to him are some that form key prophetic texts in the New Testament. Psalm 16:10 is quoted by both Peter and Paul as prophetically fulfilled in Christ's resurrection (Acts 2:27, 13:35). Psalm 110:1 is the most quoted Old Testament verse in the New Testament, and 110:4 figures heavily in the book of Hebrews as pointing to the superior priesthood Christ exercised on our behalf. Jesus himself uses Psalm 110:2 to baffle his critics concerning the question of the Messiah's identity (Matt. 22:41–46).

ANOINTED ONES

David, the great king of Israel, is one of the most important characters in the Bible. David was a powerful warrior, an insightful musician, and a hero of the faith. He is also important for his connection to Christ.

God promised to build a house for David (2 Sam. 7:8–16). God meant that David's lineage would endure forever. God fulfilled his promise with the birth of Solomon. However, the greatest fulfillment of this promise is the birth of Jesus Christ.

The words *Messiah* and *Christ* mean *anointed*. That is, when God chose a person for some task, that person would have been anointed with oil. Anointment symbolized God's choice, empowerment, and favor on the person anointed. People were anointed for specific tasks. Over time, it became clear that God's plans included a special Messiah. God anointed Jesus to be King and Savior of humanity.

All human rulers were flawed and sinful; but Christ, although fully human, was flawless: "...one who has been tempted in every way, just as we—yet was without sin" (Hebrews 4:15). Through Christ's obedience, death, and resurrection, God would forgive and make a people for himself. In Christ, all of God's promises and plans come to pass.

FRIENDS TO THE END

Among the many events that make David's life unique, his friendship with Jonathan, King Saul's son, stands out:

+ The two became friends after David's triumph over Goliath. The Scripture says, "Jonathan became one in spirit with David, and he loved him as himself" (1 Sam. 18:1).

+ The friendship was costly to Jonathan. At his own risk, Jonathan protected David on more than one occasion. Although King Saul was out to kill David, Jonathan remained true to his bond. Jonathan protected David by giving him advanced knowledge of his Saul's plans.

+ Before fleeing from Saul's court, David promised to be kind to Jonathan's descendants. They parted as friends with many tears.

+ Jonathan died in battle against the Philistines along with his father. David expressed his deep sorrow

Jonathan's Token to David by Leighton

and love for Jonathan in a poem called "The Lament of the Bow" (2 Sam. 1:17–27). The words, "Your love for me was wonderful, more wonderful than that of women," reflect this deep friendship of precious and rare value.

ATTITUDES OF THE HEART

Saul's Attitude Toward David		David's Attitude Toward Saul	
Saul was jealous	1 Sam. 18:9	David remained respectful	1 Sam. 18:8
Saul attempted to make David fail	1 Sam. 18:11	David obeyed Saul's command	1 Sam. 18:5
Saul tried to kill David	1 Sam. 19:1–24	David refused to kill Saul	1 Sam. 24:6; 26:9–12
"I have treated you badly"	1 Sam. 24:17	"You have treated me well"	1 Sam. 24:17

THE BATTLE IS THE LORD'S

- Just as Saul was tested, David needed to be tested as well.
- Saul's life was filled with fear and depression.
- When the Philistines challenged Israel, the king of Israel had to lead God's armies to victory.
- However, when the mighty Philistine hero, Goliath, challenged the Israelites to fight him, all cowered in terror (1 Sam. 17:11).
- Saul failed again to lead Israel's armies.
- During this battle, Jesse, David's father, sent David to check on his older brothers at the field of battle (1 Sam. 17:17–19).
- As he arrived and heard the commotion in the camp, David was surprised with the Philistine's defiance of God's army.
- With great courage and faith, David accepted the challenge and stepped forward to fight the Philistine.

Contrasting Warriors

The Bible's description of Goliath is important. It stands in contrast to David.

Opponent	Goliath	David
Description	Terrifying, giant warrior	Shepherd boy
Height	Nearly nine feet tall	Unknown and unimpressive
Weapons	Sword, spear, and javelin of bronze and iron; armor weighing about 125 pounds	Shepherd's staff and sling, five pebbles; a heart of faith and complete trust in the Lord

Ancient armies often allowed a fight between champions to decide the fate of the battle. However, behind the military practice was the understanding that it was not only champions fighting. Rather, the gods themselves fought on behalf of each army. At stake was more than just a battle: the name (or fame) of the Lord himself was on the line.

"Who is this uncircumcised Philistine that he should defy the armies of the living God?"(17:26).

David's answer showed his utter confidence in his God: "You come against me with sword and spear and javelin, but I come against you in the name of the LORD Almighty, the God of the armies of Israel, whom you have defied" (17:45). The battle ended before it had even started. Like many other parts of the Bible show, no one and nothing can stand against the Lord of creation (see Ex. 15:1–18).

HOW THE MIGHTY HAVE FALLEN

David's life took an unpredictable turn. David became an outlaw, escaping Saul's many attempts to kill him (1 Sam. 22:1–2). The Bible describes a difficult, if exciting, time in exile from his land. David's life went from being an independent fighter, to being in the midst of the Philistines—acting like a madman to avoid being killed (1 Sam. 27)—to serve as a mercenary for the Philistine king Achish (1 Sam. 29).

While Saul remained acting king of Israel, especially in the Northern Tribes. David increased his influence and power,

Of Fools and Fair Women

During David's outlaw years, as he struggled to survive the elements and a hostile, insane king, he must have had a difficult time maintaining the compassion and civility necessary for kingly service. The story of David and Abigail shows David's sensitivity to his own failings and serves as another reminder of what made him "a man after God's own heart": "May you be blessed for your good judgment and for keeping me from bloodshed this day and from avenging myself with my own hands." (See 1 Sam. 25.)

especially in the Southern Tribes. After Saul's death, David strengthened his position in the Southern Tribes and became king of Judah. In the North, Saul's son Ishbosheth became king over Israel (2 Sam. 2:8–9). During two years (2 Sam. 2:10), the two kingdoms warred with each other, but "David grew stronger and stronger, while the house of Saul grew weaker and weaker" (2 Sam. 3:1).

SAUL'S DECLINE AND DAVID'S RISE TO POWER

Saul	David
Saul hunted down David to kill him. The king neglected his task of protecting the land against its enemies, especially the Philistines.	David fled Saul fearing for his life. The young warrior continued to fight and defeat the Philistines.
Saul's relationships with his family suffered from the king's increasing rage.	David reaffirmed and strengthened his relationship with Jonathan, Saul's eldest.
Saul consulted a medium to conjure Samuel because the Lord did not answer him.	David constantly inquired the Lord for his next decision (1 Sam. 23:2, 4; 30:8).
Saul took his own life to avoid falling into the hands of the Philistines	David lamented the death of Saul and Jonathan. He became the king of Israel.
Saul's heir Ishbosheth was assassinated.	David executed the murderers of Ishbosheth.

DAVID'S VICTORIES

Because of his focus on the Northern territories and his obsession to capture David, King Saul never conquered Jerusalem. Since the times of Joshua, the Israelites had been unable to conquer the city (see Josh. 15:63). The city belonged to a Jebusite tribe (2 Sam. 5:6–15). The leaders of Jerusalem were very confident in the strength of the city. They bragged that even blind people could repel David's attack (2 Sam. 5:6). However, with a brilliant military move, David conquered the city and made it his own.

Conquering Jerusalem was David's first action as king of Israel. Jerusalem was important because:
1. Jerusalem was important for David as the new king of all Israel. Hebron was a traditional seat of power for the Southern Tribes. David had to unify the North and the South.
2. Jerusalem became a symbol of the unity of the kingdom of Israel. Eventually, Jerusalem, David's city (2 Sam. 5:7), became God's city as well (2 Chron. 6:6).

David's victory against the Philistines was David's second action as king of Israel. Throughout this time, David continued to inquire of the Lord for guidance (2 Sam. 6:19). God continued to give David victory after victory. Another important victory was for David to bring the ark of the covenant to Jerusalem. Although the actual transport of the ark to Jerusalem proved tragic with the death of Uzzah, eventually David brought it to Jerusalem with great celebration and joy (2 Sam. 6). Bringing the ark to Jerusalem showed David's commitment to God. The ark represented God's presence. David recognized that God himself was the King of Israel. He recognized that all authority and blessings proceeded directly from God's presence.

SALVTI
PATRIAE
ET
CHRISTIA
NAE GLO
RIAE

CAMPAIGNS OF DAVID (Approx. 1010–992 BC)

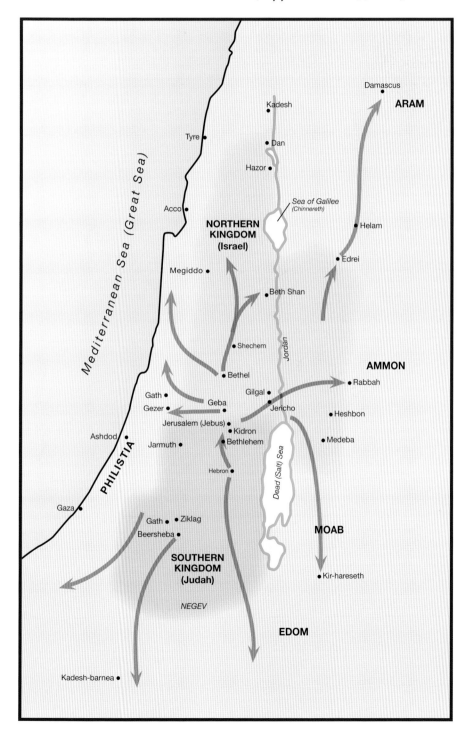

ARAM
Damascus

Kadesh

Tyre
Dan

Hazor

Acco

Sea of Galilee
(Chinnereth)

Helam

NORTHERN
KINGDOM
(Israel)

Megiddo

Edrei

Beth Shan

Mediterranean Sea (Great Sea)

Shechem

Jordan

AMMON

Bethel

Rabbah

Gilgal

Gath

Geba

Gezer

Jericho

Heshbon

Jerusalem (Jebus)
Kidron
Bethlehem

Ashdod

Medeba

Jarmuth

PHILISTIA

Hebron

Dead (Salt) Sea

Gaza

Gath   Ziklag

Beersheba

MOAB

SOUTHERN
KINGDOM
(Judah)

Kir-hareseth

NEGEV

EDOM

Kadesh-barnea

God's Covenant with David

The high point of David's life came in a moment when David experienced some peace. "The Lord had given him rest from all his enemies around him" (2 Sam. 7:1; see Deut. 3:20; 12:10; 25:19). During moments of respite, David wondered about a house for the Lord. The prophet Nathan first agreed that David should build a temple. God, however, directed the prophet to bring a different message to the king. David would not build the house of God. Rather, God would build a house for David! It was a reversal of what David expected. This reversal plays on two meanings of the expression building a house: (1) Building an actual temple ("the house of God"); (2) building a dynasty ("the house of David").

God's dwelling place

The Bible makes it clear that God chose Jerusalem, Zion, to be his dwelling place on earth. Just like he had chosen to live in the midst of his people in the wilderness after the Exodus, God chose to continue living in their midst. However, David was not to build it. First Chronicles 22:8 states the reason: David was a man of war with much blood on his hands. Instead, Solomon, David's son, would build the temple (1 Chronicles 22:9).

David's house

Another characteristic of ancient kings was that they established dynasties, or houses. The principle that the Israelite king would not be like the kings of the other nations still applied. God's promise did not intend to be merely for David. The establishment of David's house had enormous implications for God's own plans. God made a covenant with David to use his family line to bring about a change unlike any other in history. Through David's lineage, the Messiah, God's own Son, would be born to redeem the world. This promise was also God's confirmation of David as Israel's king.

Bathsheba Goes to King David by Cecchino del Salviati

Family Ties
Bathsheba also happened to be the granddaughter of Ahithophel, David's counselor who later betrayed David by siding with Absolom in his rebellion.

A King-Sized Sin

As David rejoiced in his victories and blessings, he stayed home while his troops went out to fight against the Amelakites. During an idle stroll, David saw a beautiful woman bathing and lusted after her. The woman was Bathsheba, daughter of one and wife of another of David's most trusted men (known as "The Thirty," 2 Sam. 23:34, 39). What the king desired, the king got. When Bathsheba became pregnant, David tried to hide his sin by making Uriah, Bathsheba's husband, sleep with her. When Uriah refused to do so because of his military responsibilities, David stepped up his plans. He plotted to kill Uriah in the field of battle. After Uriah died as a soldier and Bathsheba mourned him, she became David's wife. "But the thing David had done displeased the Lord" (2 Sam. 11:27). God sent the prophet Nathan to confront David. Although David thought he had gotten away with his crimes, Nathan's clever story caused David to discover and recognize his sin (2 Sam. 12:1–12).

David's sin was terrible: coveting, adultery, abuse of his authority, and finally murder. In the ancient world, kings had absolute authority. If they desired to take a plot of land (or someone's wife or house), they just did it (see 1 Kings 21). Saul attempted to act like any other king by ignoring Samuel's instructions: he acted as a law unto himself. David, on the other hand, knew he had committed a terrible sin and tried to hide it. He knew himself below God's law and accountable to it. Despite David's foolishness, God's will mattered to him. David showed his repentance by confessing his sin (2 Sam. 12:13), fasting and praying (2 Sam. 12:16–23).

Both David and Saul did great evil before God. However, the effects on Saul and David's role in God's plans were very different. Saul's rebelliousness cut him out of his role as king. David's sins brought about a terrible punishment but did not affect his role in God's plans to bring the Messiah through his lineage.

David Contemplating the Head of Goliath by Orazio Gentileschi

A man after God's own heart

God punished David's sin. The punishment was as terrible as the sin.
The prophet Nathan, who had brought great words of
assurance and affirmation to David (2 Sam. 7),
brought the dire news to the king. Because of his
violent acts, "the sword will never depart from
your house" (2 Sam. 12:10). In addition, the baby
that was still to be born would also die (12:14).
David's agony is reflected in Psalm 51. Despite
the severe punishment, God forgave David!
(2 Sam. 12:13). God's amazing grace accepted
David's repentance, faith, and regret.

*David is one of us: people who have sinned, sought, and found God's
forgiveness.*

The Sword Will Never Depart

The Bible provides sorrowful examples of God's punishment happening in
David's family throughout the generations.

Reference	Event	Result
2 Sam. 13	Amnon raped Tamar.	Absalom killed Amnon.
2 Sam. 14–18	Absalom rebelled against David and tried to take over the kingdom.	David had to escape Jerusalem. Absalom took over the kingdom and made David's concubines his. Absalom dies later escaping David's armies.
1 Kings 1	Before David died, Adonijah declares himself as the new king of Israel.	God chose Solomon as the new king. However, the kingdom would eventually be divided into two kingdoms (1 Kings 12–14).

*It is good to know that God looks deep in our innermost being, that
he knows our secrets, both the great goodness and great evil we are
capable of doing. Still, Jesus came to die for each of us so we can
become like David: people after God's own heart!*

An Inglorious Ending

After much struggle and grief, David arrived at the end of his life. Through the book of Samuel, David had been a strong man of war and authority. However, in 1 Kings 1:1–4, King David is an old man, incapable of staying warm, and out of touch with what is happening in his kingdom.

David's last kingly act was choosing the next king of Israel. Instead of choosing Adonijah, the oldest son alive (and who was already acting as though he was the next king), David chose Solomon. Although the book of Kings is not clear why David made this choice, the book of Chronicles states that God himself had chosen Solomon (1 Chron. 22:6–10).

A Glorious Foreshadowing

Through David's life, we can see God setting up history for the coming of Christ. Many events in David's life point to the life of Jesus Christ, the Messiah.

David	Christ
David was pursued by Saul, the rejected king of Israel (1 Sam. 19).	Jesus was pursued by Herod, the illegitimate king of Judah (Matt. 2:13–18).
David's enemies came after him, but were overpowered by the Holy Spirit (1 Sam. 19:18–24).	Jesus' enemies came to arrest him and were overpowered by the Holy Spirit at Jesus' word (John 18:1–11).
David had a friend and advocate in Jonathan who spoke up for David at the risk of his own life (1 Sam. 20).	Jesus had an advocate in John the Baptist who spoke up for Jesus at the risk of his own life (John 3:22–30).
David was tempted and fell (2 Sam. 11).	Jesus was tempted and did not fall (Heb. 4:15).
Even with David's imperfections, God loved David and made a covenant with him (2 Sam. 7:11–16).	Christ, in his love for humanity, made a new covenant (Matt. 26:28; Heb. 12:24).
David's son, Solomon, whose name means "Peace," inherited David's throne (1 Kings 1:29–30).	David's offspring, Jesus, is called the Prince of Peace and he holds David's throne forever (Isaiah 9:6; Luke 1:31–33).

When we see David's life in the light of this great truth, we can have hope to believe that our own lives, too, point to Christ, and joy in the Lord of history who makes wonderful stories out of us.

TIME LINE OF DAVID'S LIFE EVENTS IN APPROXIMATE ORDER. EXACT DATES UNKNOWN.

David is born (1041 BC)

Saul becomes jealous of David's popularity and success

Saul's son Jonathan declares lifelong friendship with David

David commands some of King Saul's troops

David marries King Saul's daughter, Michal

Saul tries to kill David; David lives in exile

Saul takes Michal and marries her to another man

David gathers a band of soldiers; they fight Israel's enemies

Saul and David by Rembrandt

David kills Goliath (1022 BC)

Samuel anoints David as king

Saul's armies chase David

David becomes an outlaw

David marries Abigail and Ahinoam

Nabal refuses hospitality to David

David spares Saul's life

David by Caravaggio

Abner, cousin of King Saul, supports Saul's son Ishbosheth until insulted

David rules in Hebron 7 years and 6 months (1011 BC)

Six sons born to David, including Absalom and Adonijah

David made king of Judah at age 30 in Hebron; Ishbosheth (Saul's son) made king of Israel by Abner

King Saul and son Jonathan die in battle with Philistines (1011 BC)

Samuel dies (1013 BC)

David lives among the Philistines

David spares Saul's life a second time

Ishbosheth murdered by own generals

David takes Jonathan's son Mephibosheth into his household

David marries four more wives and takes several concubines, has more children

David kills Uriah, marries Bathsheba, and repents. Solomon is born (996 BC)

Absolom rebels against his father and dies

David made king of Israel; conquers Jerusalem and makes it his capital; rules 33 years (1005 BC)

David averts plague by a sacrifice to God on what would later be the Temple Mount

David dies, leaves kingdom to son Solomon (971 BC)

David consolidates kingdom by victories over Philistines, Moabites, Arameans, Edomites, and Ammonites

God promises that David's kingdom will last forever

Celebration when the ark returns; Michal scorns David's fervor

David orders the ark of the covenant to be returned to Shiloh from Kiriath Jearim

David defeats the Philistines at Baal Perazim

David Bearing the Ark by Domenico Gargiulo

David Uriah by Rembrandt

David with the Head of Goliath by M. Stanzione

DAVID'S FAMILY TREE

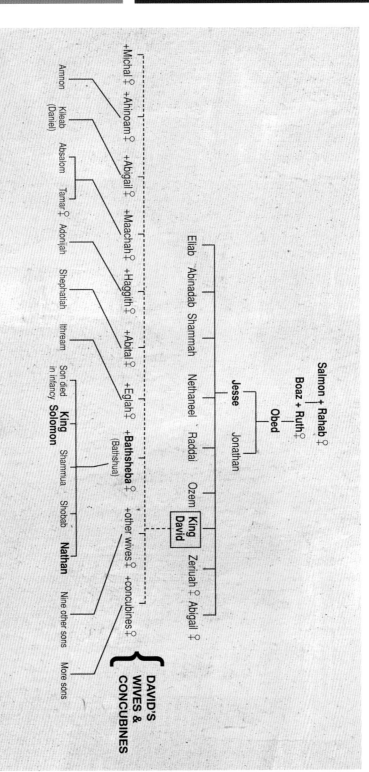

♀ = female

Bold type = ancestor of Jesus

Salmon + Rahab ♀
Boaz + Ruth ♀
Obed
Jesse

Eliab   Abinadab   Shammah   Nethaneel   Raddai   Ozem   **King David**   Zeruiah ♀   Abigail ♀

Jonathan

+Michal ♀
+Ahinoam ♀ — Amnon
+Abigail ♀ — Kileab (Daniel)
+Maachah ♀ — Absalom, Tamar ♀
+Haggith ♀ — Adonijah
+Abital ♀ — Shephatiah
+Eglah ♀ — Ithream
+**Bathsheba** ♀ (Bathshua) — Son died in infancy, **King Solomon**, Shammua, Shobab, **Nathan**
+other wives ♀ — Nine other sons
+concubines ♀ — More sons

DAVID'S WIVES & CONCUBINES

1 Corinthians 13

Love in All Relationships

Verse-by-Verse Study

The Four Loves

Love Requires Courage

Love is patient, love is kind. It does not envy, it does not boast, it is not proud. It is not rude, it is not self-seeking, it is not easily angered, it keeps no record of wrongs. Love does not delight in evil but rejoices with the truth. It always protects, always trusts, always hopes, always perseveres. Love never fails.
—1 Corinthians 13:4–8a

First Corinthians 13 is one of the most beautiful, inspiring, and relevant passages in the New Testament. Its relevance lies in the very importance of relationships in our lives. God created us to be relational beings. Relationships are not optional. They are central to what it means to be human. We inevitably relate to God, nature, and each other. Love is what makes relationships possible. Love binds people in relationships.

However, we are broken people. Sin has affected our relationships. They are not what they should be: there is distrust, pain, anger, misunderstanding, fear, isolation, and abuse. We are afraid of being hurt—so much so, that we hardly let anyone, including God, see us with our guard down. Fear has kept us from true intimacy and from deep, satisfying relationships.

© Maria Bobrova

How, then, can we feel safe to open our hearts and let others see who we are? The Apostle Paul shows us "the most excellent way" to feel safe to open our hearts to others, and to be safe for others to open their hearts to us. The love that Paul describes fosters intimacy, openness, security, comfort, growth, and support. It is a love that is applicable to all areas of our lives: from spouses and children, to people inside and outside the church, to people we meet unexpectedly, accidentally, or temporarily in our daily activities. We are safe because God has shown this love to us through Christ, and the Spirit pours it in our hearts daily. He fills us with all the love we need. It is a love that "drives out fear" (1 John 4:18).

OVERVIEW OF 1 CORINTHIANS 13

The beautiful words about love occur in the context of Paul's teachings about spiritual gifts. God gives spiritual gifts to his people for the benefit of the whole church. The Apostle shows "the most excellent way" (1 Cor. 12:31). That is, when God's people exercise their spiritual gifts in the context of love, they work the way God intends them.

1. *Gifts Without Love* = Nothing.

- Tongues
- Prophecy
- Knowledge
- Faith
- Martyrdom

© Andrejs Pidjass

2. *Definition of Love*

Love is
- Patient
- Kind

Love does not
- Envy
- Boast

    Love is not
- Proud
- Rude
- Self-seeking
- Easily angered

- Keep record of wrongs
- Delight in evil

Love does
- Rejoice with the truth
- Protect always
- Trust always
- Hope always
- Persevere always

© absolut

3. *Love Never Fails*

- Prophecy
- Tongues
- Knowledge

These gifts will end

Love is the perfect goal and fulfillment of
- Incomplete knowledge
- Incomplete prophesy
- Growth
- Sight/Recognition

Conclusion

Love is the greatest of eternal affections/attitudes
FAITH   HOPE   LOVE

THE CHARACTERISTICS OF LOVE

	Love Is...	Definition	Scripture
v. 4	Patient, steadfast, enduring	Willing to endure emotional discomfort and suffering. It is the opposite of demanding what we want right now and being easily angered.	Eccl. 7:8; Gal. 5:22; James 5:7–9
v. 4	Kind, good, pleasant	Seeking the best for the other person. Love is willing to go the extra mile. It is the opposite of being rude.	Gal. 5:22; Eph. 4:32; Col. 3:12
v. 6	Rejoicing with truth	Happy to know what is true. It is the opposite of delighting in evil. Knowing and admitting the truth creates a reliable environment for the other person.	2 John 4; 3 John 3–4
v. 7	Always protective, preserving	Love reassures others that their heart is safe with us. It is the opposite of keeping a record of wrongs.	1 Cor. 9:12; Gal. 6:1–2
v. 7	Always trusting, believing, faithful	Trust and faithfulness are necessary for an open, intimate relationship. When people open up their hearts, they need to be safe and cared for, even when they disappoint you. It is the opposite of self-seeking.	1 Cor. 13:13
v. 7	Always hopeful, expectant, confident	Hopeful that, despite sin and mistakes, God blesses our faithfulness. Hopeful that, even if other people may abuse our trust, God will always be reliable. It is the opposite of a cynical, angry outlook.	Ps. 31:24; Joel 3:16; Rom. 15:13; 1 Cor. 13:13
v. 7	Always persevering, enduring, abiding	Despite wrongs and mistakes, love survives. Love makes people available to others, ready to listen, lend a hand, or be a comforting shoulder. It is the opposite of failing or falling.	Rom. 12:12; 1 Peter 2:20

	Love Is Not...	Definition	Scripture
v. 4	Envious, jealous, covetous	Wanting to be what others are or to have what others have. It is possessiveness to the point of obsession, the opposite of *contentedness*.	Job 5:2; Ps. 37:1; Prov. 27:4; 1 Tim. 6:4; Titus 3:3
v. 4	Boastful, bragging, conceited	Constantly talking about oneself in a conceited way. It is the opposite of quiet *humility*.	Ps. 10:3; Prov. 25:14; James 3:5, 4:16
v. 4	Proud, arrogant, egotistical	Having an inflated sense of the self, having a "big head." Living as if only *your* opinion, tastes, and choices matter. It is the opposite of *being humble*.	Prov. 16:5; Jer. 50:31–32; James 4:6; 1 Peter 5:5
v. 5	Rude, immodest, disgraceful	A lack of consideration for other's feelings or needs; insolent, offensive and provocative behavior. The attitude of being more important than others. It is the opposite of *kindness*.	Rom. 1:27; 1 Cor. 7:36; Rev. 16:15
v. 5	Self-seeking, self-centered, selfish	"Looking out for number one," or being wrapped up in one's own concerns. It is the opposite of *a life centered on God*.	1 Cor. 10:24, 33; Rom. 15:1–2; Phil. 2:4,21
v. 5	Easily angered, irritable, provoked	Always ready for an argument, having a short fuse. It is the opposite of *patience and kindness*.	Eccl. 7:9; Eph. 4:31–32; Col. 3:8, 21; Titus 1:7
v. 5	Keeping records of wrong, resentful	Unable to let go of past injustices, keeping a list of wrongs, and, often, planning revenge. Reminding others of how they have failed you in the past, and probably will in the future. It is the opposite of *being kind and forgiving*.	Prov. 24:29; Luke 9:53–55; Col. 3:13
v. 6	Delighting in evil	Getting a kick out of other's troubles or the enjoyment of bad or twisted behavior. It is the opposite of *rejoicing in the truth*.	Rom. 1:32

POSITIVE QUALITIES OF LOVE

Positive Quality	Example	What to Do
Patient: Patience is the ability to deal with a great deal of distress without becoming angry or annoyed. Patience is vital for deep, intimate, significant relationships. Understanding and accepting that we all are flawed people with weaknesses, inabilities, and foolish behaviors is the foundation for patience. Being patient does not seem to be a natural quality. It takes intention, practice, trial and error, and prayer. A patient person creates the space and acceptance that other people need to blossom and thrive as individuals.	Job 1:13–21—Job was a very patient man. He dealt with a lot of emotional and physical discomfort.	Think about something or someone that "pushes your buttons." Plan out how you are going to practice patience the next time you encounter that situation.  © sonya etchison
Kind: "Giving until it hurts," is how Teresa of Calcutta defined love. A kind heart goes the extra mile to show its love. When we show kindness, we give until it hurts; we keep the other person's feelings and needs at the front of our minds. Kindness, then, becomes a way to show how much the other person means to us. Often, a thoughtful, kind word can cause anger to dissolve and allow a relationship to repair. Kind words and actions can soothe a hurting or resentful heart. They can open the door to reconciliation and healing.	Joshua 2:6–16—Rahab showed kindness to the Israelite spies by hiding them from danger. As a result, her family was saved from the destruction of Jericho.	Ask God to help you to think of several persons who might benefit from an act of kindness. Plan how you will make this happen.

"Love anything and your heart will be wrung and possibly broken. If you want to make sure of keeping it intact you must give it to no one, not even an animal. Wrap it carefully round with hobbies and little luxuries; avoid all entanglements. Lock it up safe in the casket or coffin of your selfishness. But in that casket—safe, dark, motionless, airless—it will change. It will not be broken; it will become unbreakable, impenetrable, irredeemable. To love is to be vulnerable." —C.S. Lewis (The Four Loves)

Positive Quality	Example	What to Do
Rejoicing with the truth: We are broken people, and we deal with broken people. We can rejoice knowing that despite the evil within us, God loved us and we can love each other. Truth frees us to deal with each other in realistic, compassionate, kind ways. It allows us to see ourselves the way God sees us. Then we can help each other improve and carry each other's burdens. Truth should never be a weapon to hurt others; rather, it is an opportunity to know each other better. Ultimately, rejoicing in the truth is rejoicing in Christ, who is Truth.	Exodus 18:1–27—Moses' father-in-law, Jethro, visited the Israelites' camp in the wilderness. Jethro noticed that Moses was overworked and overwhelmed. He corrected Moses and advised him to train other people who could help him. Instead of hearing criticism, rejection, and judgment, Moses accepted his father-in-law's advice. Jethro spoke truth to Moses out of love and concern; by accepting Jethro's advice, Moses showed his joy in truth.	Take an inventory of your own life. List the positive qualities that God can use for his purposes (see the lists of gifts in Rom. 12, 1 Cor. 12, and Eph. 4 and fruits of the Spirit in Gal. 5:16–25). Then make a list of areas of your life that need changing. Make an honest assessment of your character, your conversations, your use of money and other things, and your relationships. How can the truth of your life help you be a better person with better relationships?
Always protective: We are all afraid of betrayal and hurt; we need to feel safe and needed if we are to open our hearts to others. When people open their hearts to us, we must protect them with the greatest care. We show our willingness to protect them by bearing their errors in a forgiving way and by refusing to expose their weaknesses or mistakes.	2 Samuel 9—David was protective of the family of his best friend Jonathan, even after some difficult times (2 Samuel 19:24–13).	Identify some ways in which you would have benefited by more protection. Plan a way to pass on that protection to someone else.

"The LORD is my rock, my fortress and my deliverer."—*Psalm 103:8*

Positive Quality	Example	What to Do
Always trusting: Only when we trust people are we able to open our hearts and become vulnerable. Breaking someone's trust ruins relationships. Only when we are truthful can we be trusted. When we deal truthfully with each other, our hearts rejoice knowing that our inner beings are safe, that our most treasured secrets, desires, and needs will not be abused.	Esther 2—Esther was a young woman when she was plunged into royal life in Persia. During this time, Esther relied on her cousin Mordecai's advice and support. Without him, her life in the court would have been very different.	Trust grows over time. If we can be trustworthy with the small things, people will entrust us with the deep things of the heart as well. Pay attention to the ways people are offering their trust. Gossip, sarcasm, or small criticisms can wreck other people's trust in us.
Always hopeful: We will make mistakes, hurt others and get hurt. Often things look grim; it is easy to despair. However, because we can trust in God's faithfulness, we can hope that the Holy Spirit will intervene and guide us. Our hopefulness is not just optimism; rather, it is based on God's own faithfulness. It is that hope that will strengthen us to forgive, to trust again, to go on.	Ruth 1—When Naomi's husband and children died, Naomi was left with only her two daughters-in-law, Orpah and Ruth. Naomi fell into distress and hopelessness. Ruth's faithfulness and courage brought hope to Naomi.	What is your only hope in life and death? Identify ways you can be a more hopeful, confident person based on the hope you have in Christ. 
Always persevering: When we are patient, kind, truthful, protective, trusting, and hopeful, our love can weather storms that seem impossible. Since our hearts crave connections, they need assurance that the people we are connected to will be there. Perseverance does not mean that love will put up with injustice or evil. Love will do what is necessary to preserve a loving relationship.	God's love is the best example of a love that perseveres. Despite our unfaithfulness, rebellion, and offenses, God continues to love us. His love is shown in Jesus giving his life for us.	How do you make love last? Remember what led you to the relationship. Renew the commitment. Equipped with faith and hope, we can move on with the adventure of loving others and being loved.

THE PRACTICE OF LOVE

Love as Patience:
Take time to listen to someone if they have a difficulty.
Overlook errors of others when they are trying hard and when the error is not damaging.
When someone comes to talk, give your full attention. Don't take phone calls while you are thus engaged.

Love as Kindness:
Don't talk about people behind their backs or reveal a confidence even if it is true information.
Care about the wants, desires and requests of the people around you. Look for creative ways of solving them.
Be polite and respectful even when others are frustrated and angry.

Love as Happy with the Truth:
Give explanations, not excuses.
Play fair. Look for a win-win outcome.
Respectfully offer alternatives when asked to do something that is foolish or wrong.

Love as Protective:
Be loyal. Don't encourage complaints. Listen to complaints, but do not add to them.
Be honest about past actions but do not destroy anyone's reputation.

Love as Trusting:
Give people the benefit of the doubt. Treat people as though you believe in them.
Ask permission. Remember, trust is not presumption.

Love as Hopeful:
Don't complain or whine. Be as confident and upbeat as the situation will allow.
Remember, even in a bad situation, our hope is ultimately in God.

Love as Persevering:
Don't dominate or attract attention to yourself, but quietly strive for what is best.
Work hard and set the example.
Never give up. It is never wrong to do the loving thing!

© Mikael Damkier

NEGATIVE QUALITIES

Love is a difficult feeling to express in words. Exploring what love is *not* can help us to get a picture of what love actually *is*.

Negative Quality	What It Leads to	Example	What to Do
Envious: Envy destroys relationships. Envy brings mistrust and betrayal. The focus of an envious heart is itself. When we are overcome with envy, we are focusing on our interests and desires (James 3:14, 16).	Envy leads one to bitterness, selfishness, anger, and other evils listed below.	Gen. 4:3–8; 1 John 3:12 —Cain's envy of his brother led murder.	When you find yourself envious of others, try praying for them. Thank God for his care for them and ask him to continue to bless them.
Boastful: Love is not self-absorbed. Constant boasting ignores the fact that all blessings and good gifts come from God. It also ignores how much we depend on and owe others. Boasting destroys love by ignoring others' contributions to our lives. It pretends to be independent and pushes people away.	Boasting can lead to an unrealistic or false opinion of oneself. Such an opinion may lead one to belittle, dismiss, or insult others. It may further lead one to a proud heart.	1 Sam. 17— Goliath lost his head over a boast.	Try breaking the habit of boasting by talking about others' good deeds or qualities. Better yet, "boast about Jesus" (2 Cor. 10:17).
Proud: We often hear, "be proud of yourself." A clear understanding of one's strengths is good; however, pride can get out of control. Arrogance and egotism show an inflated, "puffed up" sense of the self. Love needs a realistic, honest, and open attitude about oneself.	Although pride may begin as a desire to be better, it can lead to an excessive love of our own excellence. Pride destroys relationships and leads to lack of modesty and humility, foolishness, and abusive, rude behavior toward others.	Daniel 4:28–37 —King Nebuchadnezzar was humbled because of his pride.	Ask God to give you an accurate picture of yourself. Thank him for the good things about you and ask him for help in the problem areas. Do not be fearful of having to change. Ask God for help to make those changes work.

© Monkey Business Images

Rude: A lack of consideration for others' feelings or needs is the beginning of disrespectful, offensive and provocative behavior. In our society, rude behavior has become a way to succeed or be popular for some. Rudeness hurts relationships. When we ignore feelings or needs, people feel rejected, unwanted, abandoned.	Rude behavior may begin as a reaction to a felt or real offense, a way to protect our vulnerability, to keep others away when we feel threatened. It may also try to hide over-confidence, a false sense of independence, and limitations. Rude behavior, however, causes anger, hurt, fear, and disconnection from others.	Gen. 3:10— Shame is a natural response to bad behavior. Adam and Eve first felt it when they disobeyed God. Zeph. 3:1–5— God warns against rude, shameless behavior.	If you wonder whether you have lost your sense of shame, try putting yourself in other people's shoes. How do you feel when someone is rude to you? Ask God to restore your conscience.
Self-seeking: The concern for oneself above others' needs may begin as an attempt to shore up a false self-image. Selfishness destroys relationships because we become incapable of seeing others' needs and desires. Our consuming desire to fulfill our every need leads us away from others.	Selfishness leads to resentment, anger, and broken relationships. Unless we are willing to see life from others' perspectives, we will be limited in the depth and beauty of our relationships.	2 Tim. 3:2— God warns us that people who reject him will become lovers of themselves. 1 Cor. 10:24— Paul tells us to seek after the good of others rather than ourselves.	Ask God to help you think of the needs of others. Plan a strategy for doing something for someone every day for the next week.
Easily angered: When we feel insecure, threatened, ignored, or offended, anger is a natural reaction. The emotion of anger itself is not evil—even God gets angry with injustice and arrogance. The problem is an anger that takes over our minds and hearts, lashing out to hurt the other person. This anger destroys relationships and hurts people deeply.	Feeling anger over serious wrongs is understandable. However, quick angry responses lead to more anger and, often, to verbal or physical violence. Uncontrollable anger causes fear, resentment, and withdrawal from the relationship.	1 Kings 21— King Ahab's anger led to murder and eventually the downfall of his kingdom.	Try thinking about the real cause(s) of your anger. Ask God to help you deal with those issues in a constructive way. Try finding ways to deal with the emotion when it flares up.

Negative Quality	What It Leads to	Example	What to Do
Keeping record of wrongs: Pretending everything is OK only causes resentment. It may seem easier to avoid conflict, to retreat and hide, to pretend things are well. However, until we have dealt with the deep things of the heart, we will not have forgiven. When we cannot forgive, we keep a detailed track of all the offenses the other person has done against us. Relationships cannot survive such resentment.	Keeping a record of wrongs leads to deep resentment and inner bitterness. A disgruntled heart can turn into a heart that plans evil against the other. When people reach this point, relationships are truly in danger of perishing. Forgiveness is critical.	1 Sam. 18, 19, 24 and 26 —Saul held a grudge against David that led to plans and attempts against David's life. Yet, it was Saul who lost his life and kingdom in the end. Col. 2:13–14— Jesus took God's true record of our wrongs and "nailed it to the cross." That is, he paid the price for us.	Think about what Jesus did for you. He took God's true record about your sin and paid it for you by his death. Forgiving others may not be easy, but it is the least you can do in gratitude. Try imagining that all the things that have hurt you are in the bottom of the ocean—gone forever.
Delighting in evil: Many people do not rejoice in doing evil. However, delighting in evil can be as simple as rejoicing when things do not go well for others. When our hearts are filled with resentment, anger, hatred, and discontent, it is easier to wish evil for others; it is easy to find joy in witnessing suffering and grief in other people.	When we allow our hearts to find joy in evil, to rejoice in doing or allowing what is not right, we become increasingly deaf to the voice of the Holy Spirit.	Daniel 6—The king's officers were so full of envy and hatred toward Daniel that they planned to kill him to get him out of the way. Only God's miraculous intervention prevented Daniel from dying in the den of lions.	Having delighted in or planned evil against someone requires heartfelt repentance. Only the power of the Holy Spirit can lead us back to God's gentle embrace. To restore relationships with other people and God, we need forgiveness, faith, hope, and, above all, love.

> "But God demonstrates his own love for us in this: While we were still sinners, Christ died for us."
>
> —Romans 5:8

© Dmitry Shironosov

A Word About Envy

"If we only wanted to be happy it would be easy; but we want to be happier than other people, which is almost always difficult, since we think them happier than they are." —*Charles-Louis de Secondat, baron de La Brède et de Montesquieu*

Although we often use these three words as synonymous, they are quite different.

1. **Envy:**
   a. The desire and resentment of what other people have or are.
   b. It harbors anger, ill intentions, and the hope of undoing what others have or are.

2. **Jealousy:**
   a. The fear of losing what we consider rightfully ours.
   b. It results in anger or withdrawal as means to protect the loss of what we consider precious. It may be a normal feeling; a warning signal—as in the dashboard of our cars—that tells of the danger of losing a loved one.

3. **Covetousness:**
   a. Dissatisfaction of what we have that leads to wanting to have other things.
   b. It is an offense against God—thus the reason it is in the Ten Commandments— because it presumes that we know better than God what we need and is good for us. It becomes a rebellious and idolatrous action by putting ourselves in the place of God (Eph. 5:5).

© Alan Orthery

"Christ did not teach and suffer that we might become, even in the natural loves, more careful of our own happiness. If a man is not uncalculating towards the earthly beloveds whom he has seen, he is none the more likely to be so towards God whom he has not. We shall draw nearer to God, not by trying to avoid the sufferings inherent in all loves, but by accepting them and offering them to Him; throwing away all defensive armour. If our hearts need to be broken, and if He chooses this as the way in which they should break, so be it." —C.S. Lewis (*The Four Loves*)

THE FOUR LOVES

The New Testament uses two different words to express the concept of love. Ancient Greek had four different words that express fine distinctions of the concept love. Although the differences are not always clear, they were generally used in the following way:

Agape	• In Ancient Greek, *agape* was used more generally for a general affection for people or things. • The New Testament uses the word *agape* in a special way. *Agape* is the selfless, unconditional, deep love that Christ embodied. • *Agape* is the love that God showed for his creation (Jn. 3:16), for Christ (Jn. 17:26), and for those who believe in Jesus (Jn. 14:21). *Agape* is also the love that believers should have for each other (1 Jn. 4:17–18).
Phileo	• It is also known as "brotherly love." • It is not as common in the New Testament as *agape*. • *Phileo* refers to the affection for and response to people—family and friends—or activities one enjoys (1 Cor. 16:22; Jn. 11:3, 5; 13:23; 16:27).
Eros	• This word does not appear in the New Testament. • *Eros* refers to the love, passion, and attraction between lovers. It refers more generally to romantic love.
Storge	• This word does not appear in the New Testament. • It was primarily used to describe the affection between family members—for example, the natural love of parents toward children.

The Rule of Love

"The rule for all of us is perfectly simple. Do not waste time bothering whether you love your neighbour; act as if you did. As soon as we do this we find one of the great secrets. When you are behaving as if you loved someone, you will presently come to love him. If you injure someone you dislike, you will find yourself disliking him more. If you do him a good turn, you will find yourself disliking him less."—C.S. Lewis (*Mere Christianity*)

Contributing Authors: William Brent Ashby, BT; Benjamin Galan, MTS, ThM, Adjunct Professor of OT Hebrew and Literature at Fuller Seminary.

Psalm 23

The Lord as Shepherd

Life Application

Related Passages

Psalm 23

¹ The LORD is my shepherd,
    I shall not be in want.
² He makes me lie down
    in green pastures,
    he leads me beside
    quiet waters,
³ he restores my soul.
    He guides me in paths
    of righteousness for
    his name's sake.
⁴ Even though I walk
    through the valley
    of the shadow of death,
    I will fear no evil,
    for you are with me;
    your rod and your staff,
    they comfort me.
⁵ You prepare a table before me
    in the presence of my enemies.
    You anoint my head with oil;
    my cup overflows.
⁶ Surely goodness and love
    will follow me
    all the days of my life,
    and I will dwell in
    the house of the LORD forever.

The Shepherd's Care

Psalm 23 reveals that we belong wholly to God, not only because God made us, but because he redeems and remakes us. The language of the Psalm shows how he does it.

In verse 4, the pronoun shifts from *he* to *you*. But there is also a shift from language about sheep to language about humans. Through the first part of the verse, the imagery concentrates on pastures, still waters, and sheep paths. After verse four, the imagery centers on human things— table, anointing of the head, overflowing cup. The language shift is so subtle, it is hardly noticeable; however, this change mirrors the change that takes place in people and nations that embrace God as their shepherd. Recognizing our need for God and his discipline is a humanizing experience, one of the major themes throughout Scripture.

Psalm 23 is one of the dearest passages of the Bible. This beautiful poem about God and his people speaks directly to the joys and fears of any human being. It is a beautiful reminder that the LORD is a caring and compassionate God. It also reminds us that, like sheep, we depend on God's care and provision.

The language of the Psalm comes from life in the field with sheep. For many urban dwellers, the concepts and metaphors in the Psalm are unfamiliar. By exploring words and images in context, one can better understand the message and appreciate the beauty of this favorite psalm.

The LORD is my shepherd

MEANING: God leads and cares for me.

Sheep are able to recognize their shepherd and carry on a simple relationship with him. They are docile creatures and are capable of giving and receiving affection. Care for the sheep means ownership of them. Shepherds often mark their sheep with a notch cut in the ear or by some other distinguishing mark.

APPLICATION: We are like sheep under God's care and guidance. We belong to God in two ways: We belong to him because he *created* us, and we belong to him because he *saved* us. As believers, we are called to suffer with him and bear his mark of love (Philippians 3:10; John 17:20–23).

RELATED PASSAGES:
John 10:1–18; Ezekiel 34:31

The Mark of the Christian

The Bible speaks of God's mark on the believer. Ephesians 1:13 speaks of being marked with the seal of the Holy Spirit. What is this mark? Some faith traditions, as an act of worship, use the symbol of the cross on the believer. Hand movements, oil, jewelry, and more have been used for this purpose, but these are only symbols of a deeper reality.

The mark of the Christian involves suffering (see Philippians 1:29 and 1 Peter 4:12–13). Paul indicates this in passages like Galatians 3:17 and Philippians 3:10. Jesus refers to the same when he identifies the disciple with the teacher (Matthew 10:24–25). But the mark must involve more than just suffering, since suffering is common to all humans. Jesus, in his final prayer before his own suffering on the cross, connects the suffering of the disciple with unity in God's love (John 17:13–23). It is the love Christians bear for each other while under fire that is the distinguishing mark, the very seal of the Holy Spirit (Romans 5:5; 1 Corinthians 8:3).

Shepherds and Sheep

Shepherds appear in the Bible many times. As the table below shows, the language and images from shepherding were common for people in biblical times.

Shepherds in the Old Testament	Shepherds in the New Testament

• Abel (*Genesis 4:2*)
 • Jabal (*Genesis 4:20*)
 • Abraham (*Genesis 13:2–6*)
 • Lot (*Genesis 13:5–6*)
 • Isaac (*Genesis 26:17–33*)
 • Rachel (*Genesis 29:9*)
 • Jacob (*Genesis 31:4*)
 • The Sons of Israel (*Genesis 46:31–32*)
 • Jethro's Daughters (*Exodus 2:16*)
 • Moses (*Exodus 3:1*)
 • David (*1 Samuel 16:11*)
 • Uzziah (*2 Chronicles 26:10*)
 • The Recabites (*Jeremiah 35:6–10*)
 • Figurative:
   〜 of God—the Shepherd
     (*Genesis 49:24; Psalm 23; 78:52; 80:1; Ezekiel 34:15*);
   〜 of the leaders of Israel
     (*Isaiah 56:11; Ezekiel 34*);
   〜 of Cyrus (*Isaiah 44:28*)
	• The Shepherds of the Nativity
	   (*Luke 2:8–20*)
	 • Figurative of Jesus:
	   〜 the Shepherd (*Isaiah 40:11; Zechariah 13:7; Matthew 26:31; Mark 14:27; 1 Peter 2:25*);
	   〜 the Good Shepherd (*John 10:11–16*);
	   〜 the Great Shepherd (*Hebrews 13:20*);
	   〜 the Chief Shepherd (*1 Peter 5:4*)

I shall not be in want

MEANING: My deepest needs shall be met. I need not desire more.

Sheep may develop a habit of wandering off the shepherd's pastureland in search of "greener pastures." Because they have few defenses, safety in numbers is necessary for survival. A stray sheep is easy prey and the watchful protection of a caring shepherd is crucial to sheep that have a tendency to wander. Sheep have differing personality traits and stubborn sheep may teach others of the herd to wander.

APPLICATION: We can trust in God's provision and care for us.

RELATED PASSAGES: John 16:23–27; Matthew 6:8

He makes me lie down in green pastures

MEANING: God makes me free to rest.

Sheep will not rest unless they are free from conflicts with other sheep, free from predators, free from pests, and free from hunger. The shepherd must protect the sheep from problems outside and inside the herd. The shepherd has to find feeding grounds where the sheep can eat safely—a place without parasites, predators that endanger the sheep, and with plenty of green pastures where the sheep can eat and rest safely.

APPLICATION: We can rest in God's security and provision.

RELATED PASSAGES: Matthew 11:28–30

He leads me beside quiet waters

MEANING: God supplies me with safe, life-giving drink.

Sheep need fresh, clear water, but they will not drink from waters moving too swiftly. This is because sheep are not good swimmers, especially when they are laden down with a heavy woolen coat. But the good shepherd will not let them drink from filthy contaminated pools either. He will lead the sheep to the still waters.

APPLICATION: We can drink deeply of God's Holy Spirit who is water to our thirsty souls.

RELATED PASSAGES: John 4:10–14; 7:37–39; Revelation 22:1

The Shepherd's Job
The job of the shepherd was to lead the sheep to safe pasture and to protect them along the way. The job of feeding the flock might involve removing poisonous plants or, in the case of a snowfall, pulling down vegetation from high branches. Keeping sheep from straying into cultivated fields was also a part of the shepherd's responsibility. Protection involved caring for the weak or sick, retrieving the lost, and guarding against predators.

The Shepherd's Duties	Jesus' Actions
• Leads the sheep to safe pasture and water.	• Jesus calls disciples to follow wherever he leads (Matthew 4:18–22; John 10:4–9).
• Protects the sheep from predators, pests, parasites, other sheep, and natural dangers.	• Jesus warns, intercedes and rescues (Mark 8:15; John 17:12–15; Matthew 20:28; John 10:15).
• Feeds the sheep, including removing poisonous plants and providing access to foliage on high branches or after a snowfall.	• Jesus feeds the crowds. He himself is the bread of life (Matthew 14:13–21; 15:32–39; John 6:22–71)
• Cares for the weak or sick lambs.	• Jesus cares for the sick and weak (Matthew 14:14, 34–36)
• Disciplines wayward sheep and retrieving the lost.	• Jesus rebukes his disciples and finds those who have lost their way (Matthew 14:29–31; 16:23; Luke 22:31–34)
• Protects cultivated land and crops from the sheep.	• Jesus guides his disciples in the way of caring about others (Luke 6:27–36)
• Prevents over grazing.	• Jesus teaches his disciples to be wise and harmless (Matthew 10:16)

He restores my soul

MEANING: God cares for and keeps my heart and mind.

Sheep may become "cast," stuck on their backs, unable to get up. A downcast sheep is one that has rolled over into a depression and cannot right itself to stand. In this condition, a sheep struggling to raise itself may quickly become dehydrated in the summer sun. A cast sheep is also easy prey for wild animals. Top heavy, body down in a hole, legs flailing the air, a sheep in this state is a funny sight to see—funny, but also helpless.

APPLICATION: We can trust God for the needs of the body and the spirit.

RELATED PASSAGES: John 16:33; 17:13; Psalms 42:11

He guides me in paths of righteousness for his name's sake.

MEANING: God will lead us on the right path because of his great promise.

Sheep are creatures of habit. By overgrazing, they will eventually destroy their own pastures. They must be led to new pastureland. Only the shepherd knows the best pasture and the best way to get there and he will lead them because the sheep are in his name.

APPLICATION:
We are to follow God's way, not our own destructive ways.

RELATED PASSAGES:
John 10:4; 14:6

Even though I walk through the valley of the shadow of death, I will fear no evil, for you are with me

MEANING: God knows and deals with my fears about the deadly dangers of life.

Valleys on the way to the high pastureland often have the best grass because they contain water and the sun has not dried out the grass, but they can also be places of dark danger for the sheep.

APPLICATION: We can trust God even when he appears to lead us into a scary place.

RELATED PASSAGES: Matthew 6:13; 1 Corinthians 10:13

Your rod and your staff, they comfort me

MEANING: God, your discipline and guidance make me feel safe.

Notice the change in personal pronouns—from *he* to *you*—here in the middle of the poem. The Psalmist's address to God becomes more personal. It is like the sheep's need to learn to trust the shepherd. The shepherd's rod protects and disciplines, the staff guides and saves.

APPLICATION: We can trust in God's guidance and his discipline as assuring and positive.

RELATED PASSAGES: Micah 7:14; 1 Corinthians 11:32; Hebrews 12:5–6

The Importance of Sheep

Sheep were very important in the life and economy of Israel. Here are some of the uses of sheep. The following list describes the different uses of sheep in ancient Israel.

- Food—Meat, Milk, Cheese (Deuteronomy 32:13–14).
- Sacrifices—Whole burnt offering, Peace offering, Sin offering, Guilt offering, Passover lamb (Leviticus 1:2, 3:6, 4:32, 5:6; Exodus 12:3)
- Clothing—Leather skins, Woolen clothing (Genesis 38:12–17; Deuteronomy 18:3–5)
- Writing material—Scrolls
- Pets (2 Samuel 12:3)
- Royal tribute (2 Kings 3:4)

Rod and Staff in the Bible

The rod and the staff were two essential tools for the shepherd. The shepherd carried a rod in his belt to protect the sheep. The staff served as support for the shepherd. It also was a symbol of authority. The Bible uses both tools as metaphors. Sometimes, rods are God's tools for justice or punishment. Staffs symbolize people in authority or even the Messiah. The following table shows some examples of the Bible's use of both rod and staff.

Rod	Scripture	Staff	Scripture
Moses' rod—Turned to snake and back, tool for some of the plagues in Egypt, parted the sea, brought water from a rock, defeated Amalekites	Exodus 4:1–20; 7:14–18; 9:22–26; 10:12–15; 14:16–22; 17:5–13; Numbers 20:6–13	Jacob's staff— Only possession, his trust in God	Genesis 32:10; Hebrews 11:21
Aaron's rod—Turned to snake and swallowed others, brought plagues of frogs and gnats, budded as a sign	Exodus 7:8–25; 8:5–19; Numbers 17:1–11	Judah's staff— A pledge	Genesis 38:18–26
Jonathan's rod—Dipped in honey	1 Samuel 14:27–30	Israelites' staff at Passover	Exodus 12:11
Tool of discipline	Exodus 21:20; 2 Samuel 7:14; Proverbs 13:24	Balaam's staff	Numbers 22:27
God's rod	Job 21:9; Psalm 23:4; Isaiah 10:5	Angel's staff	Judges 6:21
Oppressor's rod	Isaiah 9:4	David's staff	1 Samuel 17:14
Israel as God's inheritance	Jeremiah 10:16; 51:19	Benaiah's staff	2 Samuel 23:21
Measuring tool	Revelation 11:1	Elisha's staff	2 Kings 4:25–37
Assyria	Isaiah 10:5	Pharaoh/Egypt	2 Kings 18:21
		God's staff	Psalm 23:4
Messiah to be struck with on the cheek	Micah 5:1	Assyria	Isaiah 10:5
Messiah's rod	Psalm 2:9; Isaiah 11:4; Revelation 2:27; 12:5; 19:15	Zechariah's staff —Symbolic of Israel pointing to the Messiah	Zechariah 11:7–17; 12:10; 13:7

You prepare a table before me in the presence of my enemies

MEANING: God, you provide for my hunger even when my enemies surround me.

Often the shepherd must prepare the pasture to remove poisonous plants. Natural predators often wait at the margins of the tableland for a chance to attack. The shepherd must be on guard.

APPLICATION: We can be confident that God will take care or our needs, even when we are hated or in danger.

RELATED PASSAGES: John 10:9–14

You anoint my head with oil

MEANING: God, you take care of my bodily needs.

Flying insects often plague the sheep in the summer months. Oil is a natural bug repellant and emollient that aids in healing the skin. Palestinian shepherds used a mixture of oil, sulfur, and spices applied especially around the head. The shepherd would use this mixture to care for the sheep.

In addition, pouring oil on someone's head was also an act of hospitality (see Luke 7:46), offering a way for guests to clean and refresh themselves. The psalmist here is grateful for God's hospitality.

> ### *The Shepherd's Tools*
> - Coat or outer garment to protect against the elements
> - Oil medical care
> - Defensive weapon such as a sling, throwing stick or rod
> - Staff for guiding sheep and to aid in hiking
> - Sometimes a musical instrument (small pipes or harp) to while away the time

APPLICATION: We are to trust God to provide for the needs of the body.

RELATED PASSAGES: Matthew 6:25–33

My cup overflows

MEANING: My provision from God is abundant. The good shepherd provides more than the bare necessities to his sheep.

He is willing to take the sheep to better grazing and water sources even if it means cost and danger. Jesus was willing to die for his sheep (John 10:15). If his is willing to give his life, he is also willing to give anything that we need (Matthew 6:25–34).

APPLICATION: We can rest assured that God will more than provide for us.

RELATED PASSAGES: John 10:10; Romans 5:17; Ephesians 3:20–21

Surely goodness and love will follow me all the days of my life

MEANING: God's goodness and grace will be with me my whole life.

Sheep, when properly managed and cared for, can aid in the fertility of the land, transforming wilderness into parkland and fertile fields. The good shepherd makes blessing follow his sheep. We can see God's loving blessing on his people not only on individual basis, or for our benefit alone. Often God's blessings extend from each of God's people or from the church itself and become blessings for others as well.

APPLICATION: We can be certain that God will always be with us for blessing.

RELATED PASSAGES: Matthew 28:19–20; John 14:18

And I will dwell in the house of the LORD forever

MEANING: I shall live eternally with God.

Sheep, after spending the summer in the high pastures, are taken back to the shepherd's property in the fall and the winter. In the psalm, "dwelling in the house of the LORD" may mean to live within the realm of God's provision and protection. For Christians, it also may mean a certainty of God's love for the church (Romans 8:35–39).

APPLICATION: Our lives are secure forever in Christ, the Good Shepherd.

RELATED PASSAGES: John 3:16

Shepherding Imagery	
The use of sheep and shepherding as an illustration in the Bible is common. The use of this imagery goes all the way back to Genesis 49:24, where God is called the Shepherd. The patriarchs, whose lives revolved around shepherding, easily understood the connection between their experience with sheep and God's care.	
Old Testament	**New Testament**
God is the Shepherd of Israel (Psalm 80:1)	Christ is the Chief Shepherd
God's appointed leaders are under-shepherds (Ezekiel 34).	The elders are shepherds under Christ (1 Peter 5:2).
Moses and David were shepherds in their early careers before being made leaders of God's people.	Christ commissioned his disciples to care for his sheep and referred to them as sheep (Matthew 10:6, 16; John 21:16–17).
Foreign leaders were sometimes designated shepherds when their leadership impacted God's people (Isaiah 44:28).	
The saving nature of these leaders pointed to God's promised leader, the Messiah, to come (Isaiah 40:11; Ezekiel 34:22–24; 37:24).	He referred to himself as the Good Shepherd. He taught about his relationship to his people as a shepherd cares for his sheep (John 10:1–30).
The prophets depicted the distress of Israel without leadership or bad leaders in terms of a flock without a shepherd (Ezekiel 34:1–10; Zechariah 10:2; 13:7).	The New Testament described the people as "sheep without a shepherd" (Matthew 9:36; Mark 6:34). But it was Jesus himself who made the most use of the image. Jesus used sheep and shepherds in parables about people (Matthew 12:11–12; 18:12–14; 25:31–46).
Zechariah wrote about God's shepherd who would be struck down.	Christ himself pointed to the prophetic word in Zechariah 13:7 as referring to himself and the events around his death (Mark 14:27). Others also identified Jesus with the lamb of sacrifice (John 1:29; Acts 8:32; 1 Peter 1:19; Revelation 5:6).

Sheep as Illustrative of:

People	Individual and National	Psalm 23:1; 79:13; 95:7
Sinful People	Wayward, Foolish, and Lost	Isaiah 53:4–6; Ezekiel 34:1–19; Mark 6:34
Sacrificial Lamb	The Suffering Servant	Isaiah 53:7–12; John 1:29

Psalm 23 is a powerful declaration of trust in God. The vivid images from a very concrete, common activity—shepherding—describes a caring, tender, welcoming God. This same God is always able and ready to protect his sheep. In this song, the psalmist celebrates that he belongs to this God. The tenderness, care and protectiveness of God become even clearer in the life and ministry of Jesus. He is the Good Shepherd who gave his life for his sheep. The human needs for acceptance, protection, provision, love, and salvation are all perfectly met in Christ.

The Bible tells us that Jesus, who is the Word of God, bought us with a price (1 Corinthians 6:19–20). That price was his death that redeemed us from our own self-destruction. That means God has a claim on us as both our Savior and Creator. From the animal to the human, from people of dust to people of the living God, we are twice and truly owned by the Good Shepherd.

Shepherd Imagery Illustrative of:		
Leaders	Prophets, Priests, and Levites	Isaiah 56:11; Ezekiel 34:1–16; Zechariah 11:4–17
Kings	David and Cyrus	1 Samuel 16:11–13; Isaiah 44:28.
God	The Shepherd of Israel	Genesis 49:24; Psalm 80:1
God and Helpers	Under-shepherds	Jeremiah 23; Ezekiel 34; John 10:12–14; 1 Peter 5:1–4
Enemies	Wild beasts, Wolves, and Lions	Ezekiel 34:5; Matthew 7:15; 1 Peter 5:8
Types of Jesus	Joseph, Moses, and David	Genesis 37:2–14; Exodus 3:1; 1 Samuel 16:11–13
Christ/ Messiah	The Shepherd, the Good Shepherd, the Great Shepherd, the Chief Shepherd	Isaiah 40:11; Ezekiel 34:22–24; 37:24; Zechariah 13:7; John 10:11–30; Hebrews 13:20; 1 Peter 5:4

Contributing Authors: William Brent Ashby, BT; Benjamin Galan, MTS, ThM, Adjunct Professor of OT Hebrew and Literature at Fuller Seminary.

Rose Bible Basics:

Parables
& Other Bible Studies

A FREE downloadable version of this guide is available at rose-publishing.com. Click on "News & Info," then on "Downloads."

The **leader guide** covers each chapter of this book and includes teaching tips and additional resources.

The **study guide** includes group discussion questions, personal reflection questions, and/or worksheets.

What participants will gain from this study:
- Understand how Jesus' parables relate to their lives today.
- Learn the difference between wise and foolish living through a study of Proverbs.
- See how the stories of David, Esther, and Joseph reveal God's purposes and protection for those who trust in him.
- Discover what true love in relationships looks like from 1 Corinthians 13.
- See the Lord's abounding comfort and provision in Psalm 23.

LEADER GUIDE

Spend time in prayer before each study session and pray for each participant.

Encourage participants to follow the Weekly Bible Reading schedule provided. The reading schedule is designed for six weeks, but can be extended as needed.

In the first session, ask participants to introduce themselves to the group and share what they hope to gain from the study or why they joined this study. Introduce participants to the purposes of this study.

CHAPTER 1: PARABLES OF JESUS
Main Idea
Jesus' parables are an important source of wisdom, instruction, and solace for believers.

Teaching Tips
Begin by asking participants to identify which parables they are most familiar with, which ones are their favorites—and why. Start with the knowledge participants already have about the parables and build on that existing knowledge to introduce new material.

Choose a parable to study in small groups. (You may want to choose one from the reading schedule.) Hand out photocopies of the parables worksheet provided, and bring enough Bible commentaries and Bible dictionaries for the groups to use during the session.

Digging Deeper
The Parables of Jesus by J. M. Boice (Moody Press, 1983)
How to Read the Bible for All Its Worth by G. D. Fee and D. Stuart (Zondervan, 1981, 2003)
The Hermeneutical Spiral by G. R. Osborne (IVP, 1991)
Stories with Intent by K. R. Snodgrass (Eerdmans, 2008)

CHAPTER 2: LIFE OF JOSEPH
Main Idea
We can trust in God's power and plan during times of suffering. Joseph's story gives us hope.

Teaching Tips
As you read the story of Joseph in preparation for this session, notice how family relationships are a prominent theme. Look up these other relationships in Genesis. Take notes on the family issues you see in these stories (for example: favoritism, jealousy, revenge, forgiveness). Remember, these individuals are in Joseph's family history.
- Abraham, Sarah, Hagar; Genesis 12:10–20; 16:1–16; 21:1–21
- Jacob, Esau; Genesis 25:19–34; 27:1–28:9; 32:1–21; 33:1–4
- Jacob, Laban, Leah, Rachel; Genesis 29:16–30:24; 31:1–55

Digging Deeper
The Book of Genesis (Chapters 18–50) by Victor P. Hamilton (Eerdmans, 1995)

Joseph: A Story of Divine Providence 2nd ed. by Robert E. Longacre (Eisenbrauns, 2003)
Word Biblical Commentary: Genesis 16–50 Vol. 2 by Gordon J. Wenham (Word Biblical Commentary, 2002)

CHAPTER 3: ESTHER
Main Idea
We can have courage for dangerous times. Esther's story brings encouragement to all who face trouble.

Teaching Tips
As you read the book of Esther in preparation for this session, take notes on:
- How the characters relate to one another—their interpersonal dynamics.
- Key verses that stood out.
- How the characters change—or don't change—as the story progresses.
- The reversals in the story.
- God's behind-the-scene activity.

Before you share your insights with the group, ask participants to share their own insights from the reading.

Digging Deeper
NIV Application Commentary: Esther by Karen H. Jobes (Zondervan, 1999)
Interpretation: Esther by Carol M. Bechtel (Westminster John Knox, 2002)
Word Biblical Commentary: Ruth, Esther by Frederic Bush (Thomas Nelson, 1996)

CHAPTER 4: PROVERBS
Main Idea
Proverbs help wise people to master the art of godly living, and to discern how our lives and behaviors are connected with God's creation.

Teaching Tips
Open the discussion by asking participants which proverbs they hear quoted most often. Write them on a whiteboard or easel pad. (Encourage participants to mention the proverb even if they only remember a phrase of it; for example: "as iron sharpens iron," "pride goes before a fall," "a friend loves at all times.") Start with the knowledge participants already have about proverbs and build on that existing knowledge to introduce new material.

Choose a set of proverbs to study in small groups. (You may want to choose a set from the reading schedule.) Hand out photocopies of the proverbs worksheet provided, and bring enough Bible commentaries for the groups to use during the session.

Digging Deeper
How to Read Proverbs by Tremper Longman III (InterVarsity, 2002)
Old Testament Commentary Series: Proverbs by Derek Kidner (InterVarsity, 1964)
The Expositor's Bible Commentary: Proverbs by Allen Ross (Zondervan, 1991)
Proverbs 1:1–15:29 and *Proverbs 15:30–31:31* by Bruce Waltke (Eerdmans 2004; Eerdmans 2005)

CHAPTER 5: LIFE OF DAVID

Main Idea
Human weakness is the perfect opportunity for God's power and grace to shine. David's story shows us God's faithfulness to his promises.

Teaching Tips
Rather than focusing on the details of the stories in David's life, draw out the overarching themes. Focus on God's faithfulness. Remember, the stories of David in the Bible are not ultimately about David, but about God. Take notes on these elements:
- Kingship and Power
- War and Fighting
- Victories and Failures

Before you share your insights with the group, ask participants to share their own insights from the reading.

Digging Deeper
Christ in the Old Testament pamphlet (Rose Publishing, 2007)

"1 and 2 Samuel" by Eugene H. Merrill in *The Bible Knowledge Commentary: An Exposition of the Scriptures* by Dallas Seminary Faculty: Old Testament, pp. 431–82. Edited by John F. Walvoord and Roy B. Zuck (Victor Books, 1985)

The Life of David, Vol. I & II by Arthur W. Pink at www.biblebelievers.com/Pink/David/david.htm

CHAPTER 6: 1 CORINTHIANS 13

Main Idea
Relationships matter. Love is what makes relationships possible.

Teaching Tips
If you are conducting a six-week study, combine chapters 6 and 7. The reading schedule covers both chapters in one week. The reading schedule also includes other Psalms and New Testament passages about love.

Read 1 Corinthians 13 aloud as a group. Because participants may have different Bible translations, print out or photocopy the passage for each participant to read from. If you have a projector, you may project the passage on screen instead. (This chapter follows the NIV translation.)

Digging Deeper
NIV Life Application Commentary: 1 Corinthians by Craig L. Blomberg (Zondervan, 1995)

The Five Love Languages by Gary Chapman (Moody, 1992)

The Four Loves by C.S. Lewis (Houghton-mifflin, 1971)

The Lost Virtue of Happiness by J.P. Moreland and Klauss Issler (NAV Press, 2006)

New International Biblical Commentary: 1 Corinthians by Marion Soards (Hendrickson, 1999)

CHAPTER 7: PSALM 23

Main Idea
The LORD cares and provides for us even in times of deepest sorrow.

Teaching Tips
Read Psalm 23 aloud as a group. Use the text provided in this book as participants may have different Bible translations. Allow time for silent meditation on this passage. During the silent meditation time, you may want to read a phrase from the psalm as they are broken-down in this chapter, then pause to allow participants to reflect on the meaning and significance of that phrase. Continue until you reach the end of Psalm 23. Close the time in prayer.

Digging Deeper
Word Biblical Commentary: Psalms 1–50 Vol. 19 2nd ed. by Peter C. Craig (Thomas Nelson, 2004)

How to Read the Psalms by Tremper Longman III (IVPress, 1988)

The Treasury of David: Psalm 23 by Charles H. Spurgeon at www.spurgeon.org/treasury/ps023.htm

Feedback
To improve future studies, be sure to get feedback from the group about teaching style, meeting location, discussion time, material covered, length of study, and group size. Choose a method that best suits your group: Anonymous evaluation sheet, e-mail response or questionnaire, open discussion. (See the feedback questions at the end of the study guide.)

Note: The inclusion of a work or website does not necessarily mean endorsement of all its contents or of other works by the same author(s).

STUDY GUIDE

The study guide which begins on the following page includes group discussion questions, personal reflection questions, and/or a worksheet for each chapter.

WEEKLY BIBLE READING

Week One: Parables of Jesus
Day 1: The Sower: Matthew 13:1–22
Day 2: The Talents: Matthew 25:14–30
Day 3: The Good Samaritan:
    Luke 10:25–37
Day 4: The Prodigal Son:
    Luke 15:1–2, 11–32
Day 5: The Rich Man and Lazarus:
    Luke 16:19–31
Day 6: The Persistent Widow:
    Luke 18:1–8
Day 7: The Pharisee and the Tax Collector:
    Luke 19:11–27

Week Two: Life of Joseph
Day 1: Genesis 12:1–3; 37
Day 2: Genesis 38
Day 3: Genesis 39–40
Day 4: Genesis 41–42
Day 5: Genesis 43–44
Day 6: Genesis 45–46
Day 7: Genesis 47; 50:15–26

Week Three: Esther
Day 1: Esther 1
Day 2: Esther 2
Day 3: Esther 3–4
Day 4: Esther 5
Day 5: Esther 6–7
Day 6: Esther 8
Day 7: Esther 9–10

Week Four: Proverbs
Day 1: The Fear of the Lord: 1:7; 9:10;
    10:27; 14:27; 15:16, 33; 16:6;
    22:4; 23:17
Day 2: Pride and Humility: 3:34; 6:1–3;
    11:2; 13:10; 15:33; 16:18; 18:12;
    22:4; 29:23
Day 3: Wealth: 3:9–10; 10:4–5; 11:4, 28;
    16:16; 22:1; 22:9; 27:23–24; 30:8
Day 4: Correction: 5:11–14; 10:17; 12:1;
    13:18; 15:9–10; 29:15
Day 5: Relationships: 6:28–29; 17:17;
    18:22, 24; 20:20; 22:24–25;
    27:10, 17
Day 6: Our Words: 10:19; 11:12; 12:19;
    18:21; 25:15; 26:28; 28:23
Day 7: Work: 10:4–5; 12:11, 24, 27; 14:23;
    18:9; 21:5, 25–26; 23:4

Week Five: Life of David
Day 1: David Anointed: 1 Samuel 16
Day 2: Goliath: 1 Samuel 17
Day 3: Jonathan: 1 Samuel 20
Day 4: Abigail: 1 Samuel 25
Day 5: David Becomes King: 2 Samuel 5
Day 6: Bathsheba: 2 Samuel 11–12
Day 7: David's Decline: 2 Samuel 19:1–8;
    1 Kings 2:1–12

Week Six: 1 Corinthians 13 & Psalm 23
Day 1: 1 Corinthians 13
Day 2: 1 John 4:7–19
Day 3: Luke 6:27–36
Day 4: 1 John 3:11–18
Day 5: Psalm 23
Day 6: Psalm 100
Day 7: Psalm 138

Parables of Jesus

Discussion Questions

1. Which are your favorite parables—and why?
2. Which parables do you find the most difficult to interpret? Why do you think this is so?
3. Why do you think Jesus often answered direct questions through stories?
4. How can we bridge the cultural gap between the time when Jesus told the parable and today's 21st-century world?
5. What are some ways the parables challenge you to see your own life and actions differently?

Studying the Parables

The parable title: _____

Where this parable is found in the Bible: _____

Step 1: Read the parable.

Step 2: Examine the structure. How many parts does the parable have? Draw a simple outline of the parable.

Step 3: Note the context.
   To whom is Jesus telling this parable?

_____

   What is the setting?

_____

_____

   Did some event or question prompt Jesus to tell this parable?

_____

Step 4: Look up cultural and historical questions. When you read the parable, what questions about biblical culture or historical setting came to mind? Write down your questions and look for answers using Bible dictionaries and commentaries.

_____

_____

_____

_____

_____

Step 5: Find the main point. What is the lesson to be learned for Jesus' audience? If a question or challenge prompted Jesus to tell the parable, how does this parable address that?

_____

_____

_____

_____

Step 6: Consider how the parable can strengthen your faith and knowledge of God.

Do you see similarities between the events or characters described in the parable and today's society or your own life?

_____

_____

What does this parable teach you about God?

_____

_____

_____

What does it motivate you to do?

_____

_____

_____

_____

Life of Joseph

Discussion Questions

1. God gave Abraham some specific promises. What are some promises in the Bible that God gives to everyone who believes in him?
2. Perhaps Joseph's brothers felt they had gotten away with a clever deception. But the Bible tells us that God is the LORD of Justice. Can you think of another story from the Bible that illustrates God's eventual triumph over wicked actions?
3. In the end, Joseph forgives his brothers. What are the benefits of forgiving someone who has hurt you? Why is forgiveness often so difficult?
4. Even when Joseph did what was right, he still received punishment as though he were guilty! Jesus said, "Blessed are those who are persecuted for righteousness sake for theirs is the kingdom of heaven" (Matt. 5:10). How do you understand Joseph's story in light of these words?
5. Joseph probably had no idea that God was working in the lives of his family members while he was away, but God knew what he was doing. What is an example from your own experience in which God was working in a way that was hidden from you at the time?

Personal Reflection

1. Even in prison, Joseph used his gifts to bless others. Are there any difficult circumstances in which you can use your gifts to bless others?
2. What are some common reactions and emotions people have when they suffer injustice? How can you avoid becoming bitter when treated unfairly?
3. It is easy to become overly confident and start taking credit for the good that happens in our lives. In what ways can you give credit to God when you achieve success?
4. Who in your life do you need to forgive? Ask God to help you learn how to forgive that person.
5. How do you understand your own story in light of the story of Joseph?

Esther

Discussion Questions

1. As you read this story, what stood out to you most? What questions arose as you read the book?
2. Power is a noticeable theme in the book of Esther. How have you seen people use and abuse their power?
3. Esther was faithful and courageous in dangerous times. Why do you think God allows people to feel afraid and face danger?
4. The book of Esther contains many reversals of fortune and power. What do the reversals in the book of Esther teach about hope?

Personal Reflection

1. Think of the last time you felt afraid. What did you do in response to your fear?
2. Read Isaiah 41:13 and Psalm 27:11. What does God promise us when we are afraid?
3. What kinds of power do you have in your life? What can you do to make sure you are using your power wisely and not harmfully?
4. What reversals have you experienced in your own life? In what ways was God working through those changes?

Proverbs

Discussion Questions

1. Which are your favorite proverbs—and why?
2. Which proverbs do you find the most difficult to interpret? Why do you think this is so?
3. In your own words, how would you explain the "fear of the Lord"?
4. What does it mean to read Proverbs in the context of other biblical wisdom literature?
5. In a few sentences, summarize what kind of people does Proverbs challenge us to become.

Studying the Proverbs

Choose at least three proverbs on a specific topic. (See the Weekly Bible Reading schedule for suggestions.) Write the Scripture references below.

_____

Step 1: Read the proverbs in at least three different Bible translations. What differences between the translations do you notice?

_____

_____

Step 2: Identify any metaphors, parallelism, or other literary devices in these proverbs.

_____

_____

Step 3: Write down any cultural or literary questions you have. Use two or more commentaries to help you answer these questions.

_____

_____

Step 4: How do the proverbs fit in the larger context of the book of proverbs? Find other proverbs in the book that are related to the same topic.

_____

_____

Step 6: Identify the situations in which each of the proverbs is applicable. (Remember, not all proverbs are applicable to all occasions.)

_____

_____

Step 7: Think of one or more individuals you know who live out the wisdom described in these proverbs. How can you learn from their wise advice and example?

_____

_____

Life of David

Discussion Questions

1. In your own words, how would you describe David's personality and character?
2. What led to King Saul's downfall?
3. Why did David continue to honor and respect Saul even though Saul was on a quest to kill David?
4. How did David's life foreshadow the coming Messiah, Jesus Christ?
5. What led to David's decline—both in his family and his kingdom?
6. Why is David considered "a man after God's own heart"?

Personal Reflection

1. How have you witnessed acts of sin lead to decline or ruin? (Think of instances in business, families, churches, etc.)
2. What does God's forgiveness of David reveal about God's forgiveness to you?
3. What does it mean for you to be a person after God's own heart?
4. How do you understand your own story in light of David's story?

1 Corinthians 13

Discussion Questions

1. In your own words, explain what it means to "rejoice in the truth"?
2. Why is perseverance worth it? Share a story about a time when persevering paid off.
3. Love always protects. How do you protect the people in your life? When can protection become "over-protection," and thus not be the loving thing to do in the situation?
4. Give some examples of self-seeking (selfishness) in today's society. How does selfishness destroy relationships—personal, professional, and family?
5. What is the difference between appropriate self-esteem and harmful pride?
6. Give some examples from the Bible of people delighting in evil. What was the outcome of their delight?
7. With so many good reasons to forgive others, why is forgiveness often so difficult?

Personal Reflection

1. When do you find it easy to be patient, and when is it most difficult? Why do you think this is so?
2. Anger can be all-consuming and overwhelming. If you struggle with anger, what can you do to deal with your anger in God-honoring ways?
3. How do you balance the need for your protection and for trusting others in your life?
4. What—or whom—is your hope grounded in?

The Practice of Love

See "The Practice of Love" section on page 89. Using that model, write down in your own words specific things. What should love look like in your life? Think of specific people at work, in your family, at church, school—or particular situations and issues that you often face.

Love as Patient: _____

_____

Love as Kindness: _____

_____

Love as Happy with the Truth: _____

_____

_____

Love as Protective: _____

_____

_____

Love as Trusting: _____

_____

_____

Love as Hopeful: _____

_____

_____

Love as Persevering: _____

_____

_____

Psalm 23

Discussion Questions

1. What stood out to you about the sheep and shepherd relationship? How does that mirror our relationship with God?
2. How do we show other people that we have the "mark of Christ" on us?
3. How do you experience God's care in your life?
4. How has God restored our souls?
5. Have you walked through "the valley of the shadow of death" in your life? Share how you have felt God's comforting presence with you in any way.

Personal Reflection

1. In what ways has God led you?
2. How does God give you rest?
3. What does it mean for you to "lie down in green pastures"?
4. Are there any paths in your journey that you need to leave?
5. How have you seen God acting to favor you even when the odds were against you?
6. If you make a list of the many things you have, can you see God's hand providing for your needs, and more?

Prayer

In the space below, write a prayer to God in your own words based on Psalm 23. Then pray it to your LORD and Shepherd.

_____

_____

_____

_____

_____

_____

_____

_____

_____

_____

_____

_____

_____

_____

_____

_____

_____

_____

_____

_____

FEEDBACK

1. What did you learn through this study that deepened your relationship with God and/or helped you understand biblical teachings better?

_____

_____

2. What was your favorite thing about this study, and why?

_____

_____

3. How could the meeting location, setting, length, or time be improved?

_____

_____

4. Did you think the material covered was too difficult, too easy, or just right?

_____

_____

5. What would you like to see different about the group discussions?

_____

_____

6. What would you like to see different about the activities?

_____

_____

7. What topic would you like to learn more about?

_____

_____

MORE Rose Bible Basics

Why Trust the Bible?
Is the Bible an ancient document that has been tampered with? Has it been edited many times over the centuries and now is filled with errors? How can we know what the Bible really said when the originals no longer exist? 128 pages ISBN: 9781596362017

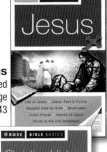

Jesus
This easy-to-understand book provides a biblically centered approach to learning who Jesus is and why his powerful message of salvation matters today. 128 pages, ISBN: 9781596363243

Christianity, Cults & Religions
This book clarifies the differences between the beliefs and practices of various religions, cults, and new religious movements. Includes topics such as: Who is God? Who is Jesus Christ? What is salvation? What happens after death? 128 pages ISBN: 9781596362024

Christian History Made Easy
This easy-to-read book brings to life the most important events and people in Christian history that every believer should know. 224 pages, ISBN: 9781596363281

Names of God and Other Bible Studies
Contains favorite Bible studies to use in small groups, church groups, and for individual study. 128 pages ISBN: 9781596362031

God in Real Life
To navigate life's tough choices, teens and young adults need a real relationship with God in their real life. This book provides clear, biblical answers to their questions. 128 pages, ISBN: 9781596363250

Where to Find It in the Bible
Handy, full-color companion for Bible study and teaching. Helps you locate: • Your favorite Bible verses by topic • 100 prayers in the Bible • Important people of the Bible • 100 prophecies fulfilled by Jesus • 52 key Bible stories

128 pages ISBN: 9781596363441

The Bible at a Glance
Introduction to basic Bible knowledge. Contains a Bible overview of each book of the Bible, a Bible time line comparing Bible history and world history, steps to studying the Bible, Then & Now Bible maps, and more. 128 pages ISBN: 9781596362000

Myth-Busters
Covers important topics everyone faces: atheism, evolution, reliability of the Bible, historical evidence for Jesus, and the teachings of "spiritual" leaders today. Great for youth and adults. 128 pages ISBN: 9781596363458

What Christians Believe at a Glance
Explains basic Christian doctrines. Includes: Jesus' claims, creeds, the Trinity, heaven. Compares 12 denominations, baptism methods, and views on Revelation. 128 pages ISBN: 9781596364141

Free, downloadable study guide *at rose-publishing.com.*
Click on "News & Info," then on "Downloads."